Kia Susan

Kia ora e hoa
Nga mihi aroha
    Ki a koe .

Travel well.
Aroha nui.

                    Gary

Thank you for sharing
the journey .

SONG of the STONE

Barry Brailsford

DEDICATION

To the ancestors who walked with wisdom and courage to keep the dream of peace alive; to all who honour the circle; to my family; to friends who walked the trails with me; to the spirit of the stone and its carvers and keepers; to the song of the stone and the hope we may learn to hear the music of the land.

GUIDANCE

The Kaumatua and Kuia, who are guardians of the old knowledge, have kindly given direction to my words by asking that the sacred places and the bones of the ancestors remain hidden, that the old lore still wrapped in the baskets of knowledge remain unopened and that the wisdomkeepers and the families remain in the shadows.

We are shaped by the touch of stone and fire to reach beyond ourselves.

CONTENTS

SONG of the STONE

Journeys on Five Trails

Five trails opened to the sacred stone and each was walked with
a companion from the animal realms.

Ka hihi
Ka kori
Ka puaawai
Ka whakaara e
Tokuu hine ngaro
Hei whaka mana ai
Ooku whakaaro
Ko te pouri tonu
Ko te po o te kori
Ka tipuu tonu mai,
Te haeata, ki te Rawiti
Ko te po o te Awatea
Mai i te Aoo Marama
Ka tu te Ao
Ka umere te Ao
Ka piki te Ra
Ki te Rangi
Tihei mauri ora!

Every stone on the journey and all the waters, forests and mountains along the way, have heard the sound and mystery of this prayer. It is a gift from Waitaha, an ancient treasure given into my keeping for the trails. I thank them for trusting me to carry it to the world.

The TRAIL of the HAWK

THE AWAKENING SPIRIT

'The smallest spark gives life to fire.'

My pack weighed me down. There were very few clothes, just what I wore and one change, a light sleeping bag and ground mat, and 25 kilos of stone. Twenty-two pieces of greenstone, carefully wrapped in cloth and destined for places unknown. I was leaving New Zealand for Arizona to meet the Hopi people and didn't know when I'd return. It might be in four weeks, four months or four years.

I was on a long trail without an itinerary. As the Kaumatua placed the sacred stones before me, he said...

'They go to those who walk with the greatest hurt and have the greatest need.'

That was my only guidance. Although I knew my journey began with the Hopi, it seemed it then opened to the four winds.

That was last night. I had just made a seventeen hour drive from Auckland to Christchurch to pack for the journey. Now I had to immediately fly to Auckland and then on to Honolulu. All this happened in two days in May 1992.

When I asked the Kaumatua if I was truly prepared for this trail, he said...

'You have just travelled around the great mountain called Taranaki and slept in its shadow. You have gone north to cut the tail of the fish. The spirit moves.
You are free to go.'

What a strange, exciting, changing life I lead. Four years before I was lecturing at Christchurch Teachers College. For 20 years my work there was in the Social Sciences, in History and Archaeology. I was soon to be honoured with an MBE for my contribution to Maori scholarship and education. I was a principal lecturer, respected in the academic world and known in the wider community for my books. I knew that world and revelled in its possibilities. It was safe, secure, predictable and very, very sane.

Now I was about to carry sacred stones to Hopiland. It was a journey without beginning or end. It was risky, insecure, unpredictable, and to some, 'very strange'. And that journey was only possible because I'd slept beneath a sacred mountain and gone to a special place in the Manukau waters to 'cut the tail of the fish'.

What moves me to write and share my life? The joy of it and the pain. I rejoice in the adventure and mystery I have been given to walk. And I still grieve for the worlds I chose to leave behind, my wife of 35 years, family life, the house I built with such happiness, friends so far away, my work as a lecturer, and the South Island with its glorious mountains, forests and rivers. After seven years of walking with 'Song of Waitaha' I want to close the circle.

Wynona, a North America Indian medicine woman, put it there for me in 1992. I had just completed the 12,000 km circle by road to the Indian Nations when I asked her...

'Should the story of the journey of the stone to the Nations be written?'

'Yes! And you must write it.'

There was a very long pause. I was about to ask another question when she said very strongly...

'But it's not the book you have already planned in your head.'

Stunned into silence, I caught the image of the book I had shaped in my mind over recent weeks. It would tell the story of the twelve keepers of the stone, those chosen to receive it for each of the Nations. I had not spoken of it to anyone. It was but a dream until permission was given to breathe life into it.

Wynona broke into my thoughts and said...

'That book is about others, you are not in it at all.'

This was true, she had read my mind, seen the very shape of my plan. I wanted to write of others. I didn't want to write about myself. I wanted to stay in the shadows.

'It is your story that is to be told. And not just the story of the long journey with the stone. No, you will write of what comes before. You will tell the story of your many journeys, the story of the spirit. And then the pains that travel through your body, the hurt that visits each joint in turn, will go from you. When you have told your story you will understand and you will be healed.'

Recently I sat with an old Maori woman who has very little sight left. Aroha saved for a long time to buy 'Song of Waitaha'. She read it with a strong light on the page and a fervent prayer to her ancestors to help the words appear. Some days she only managed one page and on very good days two. Aroha asked me to tell her a story so I took her on the journey to the Red Earth. Her enjoyment was a delight. As I left, Aroha asked if the stories could become a book, then she would always travel the trails with me.

This is my story and my truth and I share it freely. Understand that my intent is not to teach, persuade or convince, for I am the student here and have much to learn. Take from it what you will, and, if you learn something, know it is your doing not mine.

You are very welcome to walk beside me on this path. Perhaps one day we will meet and you will share your story, for your journey is part of mine and mine is part of yours.

Te Hei Mauri Ora,

Ko Barry Brailsford
Ko Tuhua te maunga
Ko Mawhera te awa
Ko Te Aka Aka o Poutini te marae
Ko Rakaihautu te tupuna
Ko Waitaha te iwi.

My name is Barry Brailsford
My mountain is Tuhua
My river is Mawhera
My marae is Te Aka Aka o Poutini
My tupuna is Rakaihautu
And Waitaha is my iwi.

This is a story of the awakening spirit. It speaks of the wairua, the spirit that moved to awaken an ancient Nation, of old prophecies fulfilled, of people of peace walking tall again. It touches the realms of the mystical where the words 'coincidence' and 'accident' are put aside. It says little happens by chance.

For some years I thought the long journey that brought me to 'Song of Waitaha' began in Te Kaha in 1970. It was there that Rusty, an elder of the Te Whanau a Apanui tribe, fired a dart into my heart. Not the feathered kind with iron tip, but the traditional challenge thrown by Maori Kaumatua, and it cuts deeper.

We were partners on the pool table and held it for an hour. New found friends. I was passing through, a guest at the hotel for the night. Tomorrow I'd work with young teachers in the local school. Rusty was old, skilled in the game and great fun. I was relaxed, the only Pakeha there but quite at home.

Just as I attempted a difficult shot he issued the challenge...

'Tell me Mr Bloody Professor?'

His voice was sharp, angry, raised to cut through conversation and compel silence.

'What are you doing to help Maori children?'

I missed the ball. He walked to the bar. The game was over. Alone, confused, vulnerable, I desperately sought a quiet exit and the safety of my room, but another voice held me.

'Stay. Don't leave. He's paid you a great compliment.'

The Maori youth who spoke stood beside me smiling. With a reassuring arm on my shoulder he delayed me until Rusty returned, drink in hand, to steer me to a small table. Tears spilled down the old man's cheeks. He wiped his eyes with the heel of his hand.

'I weep for my grandchildren. I worry so much about them and fear for their future.'

We talked and he shared his pain, his dreams and his trust. At that time this little community was sorely stretched by the demands of a changing world. I listened. There were no easy answers.

We parted. Rusty to wrap himself in the rich cloak of his heritage and the hope it would survive to serve his grandchildren. Me to seek an anchor to hold to as ancient tides swept into my life. I was an innocent. I had no way of knowing a seed sown many years ago was watered by his tears. I understood nothing of that, or of a prophecy written in the stars hundreds of years ago.

While Rusty's challenge was not forgotten, it didn't loom large in the next three years. I continued to send student teachers to train in Maori schools to meet the needs of all our children with greater understanding. I felt I was doing the best I could in the world I could influence.

Then in 1973 my life took a new direction. There was no drama in this, but in hindsight that year was a watershed. At the invitation of Canterbury Museum we took our history students to the Kaikoura Peninsula to do archaeological surveys of villages, fortifications and garden sites. From that work was born 'The Tattooed Land'. This book, which appeared in 1980 after 23,000 hours of fieldwork and writing, gave any who wished to walk the old sites in the South Island, the maps, photographs and traditions to see the story of the past. It placed value on the imprint the ancestors etched deep in the land and brought legal protection to the old places.

'Greenstone Trails' followed in 1982. This book travelled the old trails that crossed the alpine passes of the Southern Alps and highlighted the movement of the precious pounamu, the greenstone so prized by the Maori.

That was very exciting and demanding research. When the 'The Tattooed land' was launched I told the story of Rusty's challenge for the first time. I don't know if he ever heard of the work and can't begin to know if he would see value in it. For my part I was trying to protect the past, to honour the ancestors and the places they respected and valued.

After 10 years of intensive archaelogical work I felt I had finished my journey into the land. I attended numerous conferences and saw the painstaking research being done by many dedicated people. The story was being pieced together, the ancient heritage of this land was being saved for future generations. It was enough and I had made a contribution. I thought I could leave it now.

But I was very wrong. I had no understanding of what was being carefully hidden from the academic world by the wisdomkeepers of the old lore. I never suspected there was another story to be told, until I was asked to write it for the oldest of tribes, and give voice to the 'Song of Waitaha'. I was about to chart a course into the dangerous tides of forbidden archaeology.

'The truth walks the margins not the centre.'

'RETURN TO THE OLD TRAILS...'

'And you Barry
Kia ora koe.

You have been chosen to write the record of our ancestors and tell the story of Waitaha
because of your skill and the awhi you gave the people of Ngai Tahu during the Tribunal
hearings. This is not the easiest of tasks because of the things that have been hidden
away from the majority of the people. People will ridicule all the things you say and do
in the name of Waitaha.

If you accept the task you must first return to the old trails for they belong to the people
of Waitaha. You have already written of the greenstone trails. It is not going to be easy for
you to go back onto the trails but they will be opened again and the numbers will be
from the old Wananga.

Be humble, listen to the land, listen to those who will guide you through the land.

For every rule of the Wananga that is broken by you, there is a required payment. It is a
dangerous journey, it is a hard journey, you must walk it as a student.

Do not confuse the old world with the new. Write what you learn and hear in peace and
love. Learn humility and love, go in peace. Carry your cross well for it is a heavy cross
that you bear.'

Te Pani Manawatu at Tuahiwi, 1988

There were to be many surprises in my journey with 'Song of Waitaha'. One of the first was to discover that before a single word could be written an ancient trail had to be reopened across the Southern Alps.

This trail began at Arahura, a village founded by courageous ancestors who came early to those wild western shores. It followed the Arahura River deep into mountain realms of soaring beauty, and came to the Great Divide where the waters of west and east parted at the sacred lake on the pass. From there the way opened to the eastern shores several days hence.

Ngahue walked this trail knowing it ended his lifetime quest for the stone of the gods. In its waters he found pounamu, the sacred stone he had searched for in many long journeys from his base in the eastern Pacific. This extraordinary navigator and stoneworker knew these mountains and drank from these waters. And where Ngahue walked so did his companion Poutini.

Later Rakaihautu, the great explorer, crossed this pass to spend his declining years on the western coast. When his last days gathered in, he was carried on a litter, back over the pass to sing his trail songs and to die in the Birth Place of the Gods. It was his grandson, Te Waari, who laid down the lore of the trail. Then Tira and Kurawaka opened the way for the stone to be carried throughout the land.

So the history of this trail goes back more than seventy generations. Its sacredness is enshrined in the ancient name it carries, the Trail of Rongo Marae Roa, the Guardian of Peace. It is the Peace Trail.

Year after year, for century upon century, the sacred stone moved along this route. The stone carriers were both men and women, but the men walked under the cloak of the mana of the women. Women have always been its keepers.

With the discovery of gold on the West Coast in the 1860s, European miners seeking their fortune either risked shipwreck on the treacherous western shores or braved the rigours of the mountain passes to reach the workings. This sacred route became one of the miners' doorways to the riches of the western lands.

While most miners were honest men who saw the opportunity to make a better future for themselves, others brought avarice and greed to the valleys. Again and again blood was spilt in anger on the sacred trail. When the desecration became unbearable the elders asked the keepers of the trail to place a tapu on it and close the way.

By 1988 this rahui, or prohibition, had existed for well over a century. While closing the trail protected the sacred realms it meant a huge sacrifice for the people. During all that time they were denied access to their heritage, for it was only on the trails that the young were allowed to learn the lore of the trails.

Every mountain and stream along the way, and each sentinel rock that marked the journey, had its story to tell. The soaring peaks cloaked with winter snow were ancestors, great men and women, who had much to teach those of today. In times past the elders looked to the heights and passed on the story of each great one as they stood before them. They spoke of journeys made from distant shores and exploration of the alpine vastness, of courageous deeds and wisdom eternal. They taught how mountains joined the land to the stars to guide the people in this realm and others beyond our seeing. Standing by the streams they tuned the ears of the students to the music of the waters. And in the presence and the power of the sacred rocks they heard voices that sang of time beyond time.

And they were denied even more. For a hundred years the stone that brought healing to the land and the people did not move along the trail. In the old days the greenstone of mana travelled this route. There was a special power in the journey for it went again to the birthing place of the stone and felt the cold touch of the waters of the lake upon the pass. When it eventually reached the coast it was ready for its journey to other places and other lands far beyond these shores. Some sailed on the great double-hulled waka, and some was carried on the land trails to nourish the Earth Mother and bring healing to the villages along the way.

It was time for the stone to be taken over the mountains again. In December, 1988, a party was called to walk the Peace Trail to lift the tapu and remove the rahui that had closed it for so long. Only when this was done could the kete of knowledge be opened and the sacred histories of the ancestors be shared. The footsteps of the walkers would span far more than an island. They would echo down the ages to join with the ancestors and ahead in time to the unborn to open doors to many realms. Young people would be taught the lore of the mountain trails. Once again the sacred places would hear the songs of those who honoured the wisdom of old and the spirit of the land. Life, long dormant, would awaken and the 'Song of Waitaha' would become a reality.

Before I tell the story of that journey I need to backtrack a little. Early in 1988 Ngai Tahu invited me to support their land claim before the Waitangi Tribunal by presenting evidence on Maori trails. I was invited to a meeting where their legal experts asked for assistance in putting traditional evidence before the Tribunal. Waitaha answered their call. They shared their 'hidden knowledge', the lore of the seas and the land, the lore of the trails and the tides, the lore of the gardens and the stone.

That was my introduction to the sacred knowledge of Waitaha. They underpinned my archaeological evidence for the Tribunal with the most ancient of markers. I was overwhelmed by the richness of this storehouse of knowledge. The day Waitaha entered my home my life changed forever.

Although my initial commitment was to present evidence about the trails, eventually it went far beyond that. When I saw Ngai Tahu's need to summarise their case in a highly visual way, I spent some weeks creating more than fifty overhead projector maps and diagrams that allowed the evidence to be presented layer upon layer. I was to spend many days hunched over the projector flipping the coloured overlays in time with the spoken word.

When I gave my evidence Pani Manawatu, the Chief of Tuahuriri Ngai Tahu, came to hear me speak of the trails. He was very frail. Some say it was the only time he attended the hearings. I don't know about that but I do know that in the days that followed he asked me 'to write the dream' of the ancestors. Born to the ancient line of Waitaha he was perfectly placed to open the way for the story of the old tribes to be told.

We all knew this wonderful elder as Uncle Barney. While his gentleness and wisdom is legendary, few will ever understand the courage he displayed in deciding to ask for the old knowledge to be written and shared for the first time. I believe two things helped him make this remarkable decision.

First he was deeply hurt by the pain created by land claims. He saw tribe clashing with tribe in cross-claims, family pitted against family, Maori in conflict with Maori; and Pakeha anxious that lands held for generations would be seized. The best and worst of our peoples was laid bare. His concern was for the children of the land, for the children of all races, for the nation.

Uncle Barney decided to look to the wisdom of the ancestors, the sacred knowledge hidden in the land, to help our children. He knew this taonga, this treasure beyond price, would give inspiration and hope to the next generation. Later I was to find the words that expressed his vision best for me.

'When we lose our story we lose our dream and
when we lose our dream the spirit dies.'

The other reason for his decision was written in the stars. Centuries ago, when warriors sailed out of the Pacific to destroy the Nation of Waitaha, the people were told of the dark days ahead. They were urged, before all else, to hold the sacred knowledge safe. It was the treasure, the taonga that enshrined the blueprint for a world of peace and light. They were told that even when all seemed lost, it was not so, for the day would come when the taonga would be revealed once more. The new dawn would be heralded by the stars. When they aligned in a very special pattern two things would follow...

First, the most sacred of knowledge held safe over countless centuries would be shared with everyone.

Secondly, the people of peace would stand and walk tall again. The world would enter a time of nurturing and caring.

It became apparent in 1988 that the stars were forming the shape foretold centuries ago. The prophecy written in the stars, the need of the people and the courage of Pani Manawatu joined to open the way for 'Song of Waitaha' to be written.

I had no idea of what the old one was setting in train or any conception of what he was allowing to be revealed. If I'd known the path that was opening I'm not sure I'd have been brave enough to take the first step. It seemed I was just being asked to write a book, to tell the story of this land from the early days. I thought I was safely wading in the shallows when in reality I was already out of my depth and plunging into deeper waters and unfathomable tides.

But how could I know the elders were about to release a story that would add a thousand years to our past? How could I begin to imagine the changes I would experience in my life when the way to the sacred knowledge was opened to me? The journey was not that of a writer but a Tohunga. Others were trained from birth to walk that path. I was untrained and Pakeha.

In the years that followed I asked again and again, 'Why me?', and it was always a cry of anguish. Perhaps within these pages I will discover the why of me. As Wynona said, 'When you have written your story you will understand and be healed.'

Looking back I see that the lifting of the tapu on the Peace Trail conveniently coincided with a New Zealand 1990 Celebration request to organise a commemorative walk over a greenstone trail. It was to be a journey to challenge the youth of this land. The party I led in November went to investigate the possibility of using this trail. Originally I planned for five to go because the huts slept six in comfort. At that stage I had not heard of the lifting of the tapu, I didn't even know it existed. Everything was 'as usual', 'ordinary', 'safe'. The book was just a book, and the trail was just a trail. One of the many I had walked over the years.

Then with a quiet inevitability this changed and I began to suspect I was indeed being introduced to another world. Something beyond me was guiding all that happened. I became increasingly aware of that.

A month before departure nine people of standing said they were making the journey. Within two weeks most had other matters of greater need to attend to and we became two. I began to look for the other three who would give us our party of five. As I went about my work a name intruded into my thoughts and with a 'strange certainty' I contacted that person and asked them to do the walk. This happened three times until I had my five. With relief I began the final organisation for the journey.

That 'strange certainty' was to gradually become more and more important in my life. We all experience it from time to time. Some call it intuition and gift it to the domain of women, with good reason, because they are often more open to its messages. I was frequently aware of this insistent voice but usually found 'good reasons' to be 'sensible' and let it slip by. This time I acted on it.

Then the unthinkable happened. Other names began to crowd into my mind, uninvited. Two came at once with such urgency I was compelled to ask them to make the journey. Now we were seven but I felt we could cope in the huts with a bit of a squeeze. My ease was broken by another name that arrived to fill my days and nights, and again I went with the feeling and we were eight. At this point I really stepped out in the tide that now flowed so strongly through this journey. My intuition was open to whatever followed.

When I looked at those who were called to this trail I realised very few of them had ever been into the wilderness. With this party of eight I needed experienced alpine people to ensure their safety. I needed the support of my two sons. Pete, who had worked at Mount Cook for seven years, was a qualified alpine guide trained to get clients safely to the top of our highest mountains. Gordon, who was working with the Institute of Nuclear Sciences in Wellington had long tramping experience and training for work in snow. I could seek none better. Together they would add a huge strength to the party even if it meant we were now ten.

I was beginning to learn, 'You can't push the river'. Somewhere within me I found the space to accommodate the unseen forces that were beginning to shape this adventure. Letting go, accepting without understanding, stepping out without knowing the final destination, recognising and listening to a voice within that was growing stronger with the trusting. These were the lessons of that month. A new world was opening before me and within.

Early in November I received a call from the Kaumatua for the trails. Would I be available to go to the Rakaia Gorge for the night at the time of the full Moon? He wanted Derek and I to be there for a little ceremony to help Richard with his work on the old Maori flutes. He said...

'The music of the winds playing in the Gorge will ease Richard's pain. It will bring understanding and open old worlds to him.'

He closed by adding, 'And you and Derek can be prepared for the work on the book.'

Richard was a Pakeha of Scandinavian ancestry, a tall Viking, who had dedicated his life to help save the knowledge of the old Maori musical instruments. Sometimes he was given a hard time for his efforts. Derek was the art director for 'Song of Waitaha'.

We travelled for an hour to reach the Rakaia Gorge. And in the next 24 hours went into a timeless space, into realms where yesterday, today and tomorrow meet as one. Everything had been prepared without fanfare. I was learning this was the Waitaha way. Now I realised we had come to this sacred place for our initiation into the tribe, for our dedication to the kaupapa, the work of bringing the old wisdom to the world again through 'Song of Waitaha'.

In the tohi ritual that began in the dawntime I felt I had stepped into a river of the soul, a place between the worlds. Thus began the long journey that would prepare me to hear the sacred words of the ancestors.

This was the first time I met the Kuia for the trails. Her whole being spoke of the people of the mountains. So I said to myself, 'Here we go again', and invited her to walk with us. Now we were eleven and that was not enough. Deep down I now knew the number had to be twelve. However, I checked this out with the Kaumatua and he said with a gentle smile...

'Twelve would be a good number.'

In calling the last one I learnt many lessons. Wanting to include a strong young man from Westland, I asked his mother a simple question, but one filled with meaning...

'Is he of the mountains?'

She said he was, but if I'd trusted my inner voice I'd have probed deeper with further questions. Keen to complete the party I issued the invitation. That was both a terrible mistake and a wonderful blessing.

Vastly relieved, I gave the list of twelve to the Kaumatua for the journeys. At first he was delighted, then he came to the last name and was felled by the weight of it.

'You have called a Whale to the trail!' he exclaimed. Silence. It was as if he couldn't believe his own words. They were repeated slowly, 'You have called a Whale.'

In my ignorance of the lore I had blundered. I had no idea why he was so upset until he found the strength to speak again.

'He is of the Whale People. The Whale People have never travelled that trail. They are of the oceans not the stone. How can this be?'

He was thinking aloud. Questioning the ancestors, the architects of the dream, and asking them why this had been allowed to happen. I failed to see the problem. I had asked the lad to come and would call him and say I had made a mistake. But he explained that was not possible.

'Those who are called to the trail leave it by their own choosing. It is out of our hands. Somehow we must find a way to open the doors for this Whale. It will test us to the limits of our being.'

This was very upsetting. I'd felt pretty good about getting the numbers right but at the very end I'd laid a huge burden on the elders. For each walker on the trail an elder would fast throughout the journey. Their karakia, the prayers chanted hour by hour, would sound out our footsteps on the earth. We would walk in their strength. Now I was asking them to find the means to move a Whale where a Whale had never moved before. It was a very trying situation for them and for me.

As we came to the final preparations life became very fraught. I was falling into that 'Why me?'

accusative phase. I was the Pae Arahi for the journey, the Trail Maker who chanted the karakia to open the trail, who lit the dawn fire to honour the spirit of the trail, who 'flew his mind' ahead of the people to find the path. At times I felt I wasn't up to all this. In the past those who led the stone carriers over the alpine passes were called to the trails by their birth stars and dedicated to the journeys as children. Years of training in the lore and the sacred ways followed. And even then not all lasted the course.

'Why me?' was answered with, 'What you need is within you. Listen to your heart. Let it be your guide. The time for talking is over. It is time to do it.'

So I got on with the task. I learned the karakia, the lore of the trail fires and the stones. But I had no idea how I would find the seven doors along the trail that were closed by the tapu placed there so long ago. Each door was marked by a rock and each defined a day's travel. It seemed an overwhelming challenge. We were soon to set off on a mountain trail to find seven sacred rocks with a whale in tow.

Put that way I was reduced to laughter. When I thought of the whale I fluctuated between moments of deep concern for what was laid on the elders, and spasms of laughter. My mind would fill with a cartoon image of me trying to push an enormous whale across a mountain pass. That picture was a great tonic. There was relief in the absurdity.

When it was time to leave, a huge surging energy coursed through me. I'd been visiting the gym regularly over the previous three years doing circuit training and lifting weights. It was as if I'd been preparing my body for this journey all that time. I felt great. But this was different. It was as if parts of my brain had been rewired. New connections made to make me more complete, to harness power that lay dormant until now. I was so moved by this that I said to the Kaumatua I thought responsible...

'You have done something to my mind, released something within me.'

'That is true, but it is not something that is not of you. One day you may do it for yourself.'

This energy was a beautiful thing. While it added physical strength, sharpened my awareness and brought great inner harmony, its abiding presence was one of all encompassing love. I felt as if every cell in my body was singing. It was to remain with me for some months and returned several times in the years ahead when great challenges were to be met.

Now the wairua was moving, the spirit of the trails was bringing everything together with great momentum. Two nights before our departure I was awakened at two in the morning by the noise of a very happy party. I looked out the windows to find the neighbours' homes were cloaked in darkness. The party was in my home. I lay in bed hearing doors opening and closing, footsteps going from room to room, laughter and distant conversation. It became too much so I went out to the living area to investigate. Nothing. No party. Silence.

It was a beautiful moonlit night so I decided to sleep on the conservatory couch. Once I'd settled in the 'party' began again so I accepted the visitors, said they were most welcome to share this home, and went to sleep. The next morning Rod, my youngest son, who was sixteen, came to breakfast with the quiet comment, 'Someone had a great party here last night'. We were the only two at home so it was a relief to know he heard it too. The elder's only comment on this episode was, 'The Old Ones paid you a visit .'

The day before we were to leave, Dora stepped on something sharp in her home and cut her foot so badly she could not come. To restore the numbers to twelve, I asked a lecturer at the Christchurch Teachers College and she moved heaven and earth to make the deadline that changed her life.

Dawn on the sands of South Brighton. The walkers gathered with family and friends for the karakia to begin the journey. The beautiful carved tokotoko for this trail was placed in the sand and a circle drawn around it with pounamu to mark the place for our feet to meet. It was a tight circle that bound us as one. Within its confines each walker was blessed with water. Then I wrenched the tokotoko from the sands and said the karakia to carry our footsteps from that shore to another.

The words came to me with great power and I sent them strongly into the world. Yet when we left the circle those who stood outside it said they had not heard a single sound. We had been surrounded by a 'cone of silence'. This phenomenon has occured many times since then. In hospitals when the karakia has been said for a patient in a crowded ward, in public places where it was but for a few, and in the mountains of Arizona when others stood outside the circle. I don't consciously invoke the wall of silence but I am not surprised when others tell me it has happened.

Our vans took us across Arthurs Pass to the Arahura River in Westland. We honoured the waters by walking into the river. Then, on the sands built up by the flood tides, we joined hands within the circle and offered up the karakia for the trail. In doing this I made a mistake. It was a simple reversal of a hand hold but it placed us all in the stance of the warrior instead of the peace maker. It was a mistake I was to repeat each day when we formed the circle to bind our strength together. And I remained completely unaware of what I had set in train until told at the end of the trail.

In ways that defy scientific explanation the elders knew of this mistake the moment our hands joined that way. They were bewildered by this turn of events. It sent a shudder through ancient lore and traditional ways. This Pakeha they had entrusted with the Trail Maker's role was unknowingly bringing a new concept to the journey. His party of twelve were walking the peace trail as warriors.

With the way open to the trail we went to gather pounamu from the Arahura River. I sat and watched the walkers wander over the riverbed and drift apart. It was a time of solitude. Anxiety, excitement and mystery filled me to overflowing. I wondered what lay ahead for our party of twelve. How would I cope with the lore of the trail, the responsibility of leadership, the uncertainty of the journey and the depths of the unknown? How would those who were new to the mountains meet the physical demands of each day and relate with each other?

Walking this wide expanse of flood-born boulders freed the mind to timeless realms. These rocks began their journeys hundreds of millions of years ago as part of the distant mountains. Soon they would be carried to the ocean to answer the call of other tides, to be bedded in strata destined to rise again as mountains. The beginning and the end are indeed one.

Each of us walks the river to find pounamu to carry over the trail. The old ones say we dream the stone. It seeks us out, calls to us, cries to be seen amidst the vast jumble at our feet. When we hear the song of the stone we answer and become companions for the journey.

I look around. Some walk with the joy of those who have heard their stone's call. They hold their pounamu aloft, cradle it to themselves and know the excitement of the dream. Others are asked to wait to hear the song, to learn to listen. Head down they wander further afield wondering why they still see and hear nothing. Going to those who seem most concerned, I suggest they sit down and wait on the stone. Let the quest go, free the mind of anxiety, still the urgency within and just wait. And they do. And they too hear the song.

We gather. Each has a stone. It is already a treasured friend and in the days to follow it will take on great beauty as it is polished and oiled by the light of the campfire. For the first time in over a hundred years pounamu is to be carried over the old trail. Where pain and anger blooded the path, nurture and love now moved to heal.

It is late in the day when we finally step out. I am concerned to find the first of the sacred doors, to lift the tapu at the rock that marks its presence, and pass through to the camping place before night descends.

How was I to find the first of the doorways shut by the Tohunga in the last century? I had visions of the party spending days wandering up and down the trail, rock hunting and saying, 'Is it this one, or is it perhaps that big one over there?'

Then a wonderful thing happened. When we rested for the first time the Kuia brought fifteen year old Puke to me. With great enthusiasm Puke explained he saw a strange and wonderful picture in his mind. He said somewhere ahead of us was a bend in the river, and standing above it, on a rocky ledge, was an old man wearing a feathered cloak. I asked him to stay in the front and walk beside me. Within twenty minutes we came to a place that perfectly matched his description. Puke had never been on this track before. Somehow he was sending his mind along the trail and linking with times long gone.

Puke's gift of mindsight existed to aid our journey. So I took the plunge and explained to him I was desperately trying to find a very special rock I had never seen.

'Do you think you could help. Would you like to try to picture it in your mind?'

His answer was to step out into the river and stand on a large rock and close his eyes. Within seconds he bounded back and seized a piece of driftwood and began to draw a map in the sand with rapid strokes. Talking quickly as he worked he described in great detail a scene that swept into his mind.

'The track curves and rises alongside a cliff-face covered in bush. Uncle Barry, you are twenty yards ahead, and looking back to Auntie and Derek who are standing beside a giant nettle. They are resting and talking.

There is a little stream that goes tinkle, tinkle, tinkle. And a river flows beyond it. The rock is there.'

Impressed by his certainty and excited by this demonstration of a power that spoke of things so ancient, I asked why he stood on the rock in the river.

'Because that's what the Kaumatua showed me to do. As soon as I had my pack ready, he took me to a rock and asked me to jump up on it and close my eyes. He asked what I could see. I said there was a valley with a fast river. Then he told me to stand on a rock if I wanted to see the way ahead.'

We seemed to walk for hours and I still hadn't found the gateway. The Sun was soon to set and a light rain fell. I turned and looked back down the track and saw Auntie and Derek resting beside a tall bush. It was a giant nettle, the first I had seen so far. I was slow to understand what was happening. Then Puke rushed up to say...

'This is the place. There are the covered cliffs, see where Uncle and Auntie stand, listen to the little stream that goes tinkle, tinkle, tinkle. This is it.'

'Take me to the rock,' I asked. But Puke set down his pack and sat on the grassy bank and replied, 'No! I've found the place, it is for you to find the rock.'

The doorway stood before me. It was merely 50 metres further on beside the big stream. Help had been provided to meet the need. Puke brought a wonderful gift to the trail. As I looked over the party I began to understand that each and every one of them was here by design. There was nothing random or happenstance about their call to the trail. Even the whale's presence would take on new meaning.

When the tapu at that sacred door was lifted and the way opened for us, I introduced each of the party to the sacred rock. Their names were recorded there for all time, to be joined with the stone carriers of ancient days. We sang to the stone and remembered those who had walked this way before, ancestors of great courage and mana. Then, after eating a little smoked eel to bring us back to the realm of people, we moved on and found the hut a short walk away.

Night gathered over the land. The trees stood dark against the moonlit sky. The first day on the Peace Trail was over. We pitched our tents on the grassy terrace, prepared much needed food and rested our tired bodies. It was a time to reflect, to remember that while we satisfied our hunger, there were others we had never met, who fasted to ensure we might walk in safety.

Day two. The dawn light touched the hills. On the terrace beside the small hut we joined in the close circle and gathered strength to ourselves and shared it with each other. On this trail twelve walked as one. As we prepared to leave Puke came to me and said...

> 'I have been to the river to stand on a boulder to help you find the next door. I did not see a large rock but I did see the dead branches of a tree standing against the sky. If you see that you will have gone a little too far.'

I knew the rock we sought this day was the most difficult of all to find because it was so small. The original one had been carried away by a landslide and was too dangerous to reach. This small sacred marker was the place from which to greet and honour the old one. I would recognise it by unusual markings that ran through and across the surface. That was helpful but it still left me trying to locate a rock no bigger than my body in a kneeling position. With Puke's vision of that dead tree in my mind, I scouted far ahead of the party. Everything was falling into place as I passed three small streams given as a guide but the rock remained hidden. Then I looked to the left and saw a huge dead tree spreading its branches wide. I backtracked a little and there was the rock, even smaller than I imagined, but unmistakable with its special markings.

During this day the track climbed high above the Arahura River. We could still see it far below, but the music of its fast waters was no longer part of our world. Now the songs of the forest quietly entered our lives. Bird song, the wind in the trees, footsteps beating on the soft earth, the pattern of our breathing and the drumming of our hearts as we laboured up the steeper grades.

Then other sounds began to filter through, exciting and unusual sounds, the music of days long gone. At first they only reached the ears of the few who were closely attuned to the old songs.

We stopped to listen. Others began to hear the music of the trail, the distant sounds of waiata and flute. It felt as if we were accompanied by many others, a joyous crowd of people who were completely at home here. It took me back to the 'party time' on the eve of the walk, to that strange disturbance that filled my home with laughter. It was the same.

The voices were muffled, just beyond the trees or around the next turn, but never in our midst. It was as if we were walking in 1988 and 1288 and 588. Somehow the veil of time was folding back on itself. Yesterday and today were joined. It felt as if the walls of time were either very thin, or nonexistent, on this trail.

Trying to understand the dimensions of time became very important for me in the months ahead. So much happened that defied the accepted views of linear time - the yesterday, today and tomorrow sequence just didn't fit the world we were walking. I was beginning to understand why the walkers had been asked to give up their watches. We were entering a different realm. Over the following days I discovered it took two and three times longer between huts than I had expected. Even when we set a good pace, and that was often, the time factor just didn't fit. I know bigger groups are always slower - but this slow? Did time slow down and speed up? Was it necessary to take that extra time to heal the pain left on the trail?

When I came to the trails again in 1990 there was an incident that reinforced my conviction that time expanded and compressed. On this occasion it sped up. We were on a training exercise on the West Coast and I had left a group of five or six sitting on a bluff while I walked back to make contact with others who were coming through. They saw me round a bend, disappear from view for a second or two, then reappear hundreds of metres further on. I wore a bright yellow parka and carried the tokotoko stick and was very easy to identify. At that moment I remember I was concerned to reach the slower group but had no sense of a shift in time. Their excitement about the occurrence was very real for they were puzzled and amazed. Later elders confided such shifts were not only possible but were still used by a few with the power today.

To return to this trail. Something else happened that day to challenge my perception of reality. We were perhaps 2,000 feet above the river and occasionally it came into view far below. I kept glancing down, enjoying the drama of its waters rushing seaward. I came to a place where the view to the river was particularly beautiful because it was framed by the overhanging branch of a tall tree. Suddenly the whole image changed. It was as if someone had placed another slide in the projector. The overhanging branch still filled the top of the frame to anchor me in the reality of what I had just seen, but everything else was gone. The river had disappeared and was replaced by three dark pools of water surrounded by rushes and backed by ferns. There was great stillness for the waters were like black obsidian, glassy, impenetrable. All this was but a few yards away.

The moment I found my voice to cry, 'Look at that!', the image vanished and the view to the river far below reappeared. Everything was as it had been. Normal. I was stunned by this changing picture.

I have never asked for help to understand this 'vision'. When the journey ended there seemed so many things that were more important or easier to handle. I definitely felt exhilarated by the image, very excited, it was one of those 'Wow!' moments in life. A gift that said, 'Enjoy the magic, we are with you.'

Did the pools stand for the three kete of knowledge, the three baskets of wisdom brought to earth by Taane Nui o Rangi? According to the teachings he flew the trails to the stars to bring the Knowledge of the Universe to the people. We were walking to open the way for the old wisdom to be shared with the world.

Why images of water? Everything is bounded by water - it is the life bringer. Life was returning to the trail as we carried the healing stones and sang to the sacred doors. Twelve walked the old ways again.

Why were the pools so still and dark? Stillness is the way to wisdom. Only there do I find the space to tune into myself and the world around me. Did the impenetrable darkness speak of wisdom held deep within the waters and the land?

Further down the track I began to wonder if it was some kind of warning. That was my 'worry meter' switching on. I was so unsure about the protocols of the trail, so concerned to get them right that it was having a field day.

Perhaps I created the image for my own enjoyment. By this I don't mean I simply closed my eyes and made a pretty picture. No, the image was 'real', my eyes were open, my mind was focused and the pools did appear and disappear. Perhaps the gift I received that day is in these words. 'Enjoy the magic, it is within you. Indeed, within us all.'

The day was already very long when we left the track to descend to the river and the hut. The height lost would have to be recouped tomorrow. The clouds closed in and it began to rain and continued to do so throughout the night. We were a happy band of travellers. I marvelled at the uncomplaining nature of the younger ones who were new to mountain trails.

Puke we have met. He was fifteen and had never been backpacking before. Yet he was so strong, so at home in the wilderness. From the moment we began he found a deep connection with the land and the ancestors. It was wonderful to see him so complete, so sure of his place in the world and so equipped to help us with the journey. Before the walk he was 'lost', in trouble, unsure of his path in life. After the trail he 'lost' himself again for a time. Does our world have a place for the Puke's of today?

Katrina was thirteen, tall, strongly built, athletic and forever calm and smiling. The trails were her heritage, for her ancestors walked here and carried the ancient wisdom forward into this century. She brought the gift of 'visions of what was to come'. When she voiced a concern I accepted it without hesitation. I knew she touched into truths beyond our seeing, and knew she saw around her ancestors hidden from other eyes. Katrina found her challenge was to learn to trust her 'visions of tomorrow'.

Pere at sixteen years was tall, slim and full of clever words, laughter and song. A musician of great ability, he brought a lightness to each day that lifted our spirits. Before we departed, the Kaumatua said Pere would be able to help me find some of the sacred doorways. However, when I asked him of this in the first days he said...

'I know nothing of the trails. I can't help you find the places you seek.'

He was as confused by my question as I was by his answer. That was to change when we reached the alpine heights, and in that change I was to learn a great deal about how the ancestors imprinted the sacred knowledge into the young.

Petariki was a bundle of surprises. He was eighteen and powerfully built, an athlete who was to become a dancer. Quiet, gentle, confident in his abilities, he melded into the party with great ease. Because he joined us on the West Coast side I never got to test the weight of his pack until we were well down the trail. It was very heavy. To our delight we discovered his main burden was an abundance of wonderful food. His gifts were many. He moved through a strange land with quiet courage.

Caroline, the last of the five teenagers, was sixteen, had some tramping experience and was very good at many sports. Derek, her father, was the art director and book designer for 'Song of Waitaha'. Caroline's story was about to unfold, it awaited us on the morrow.

By the end of day two we were finding the pattern for the walk. I went out in front seeking the easiest route when the trail was not clear. Pete and Gordon were the kaiarahi, the trail guides. Pete led the party, set the pace for it, handled the river crossings, the rope work, decided on the resting places and looked to the safety of all. He was so at home in the mountains, and so confident in his ability to meet his own needs, he was able to completely dedicate his attention to the others. Not many of us attain that skill in the wilderness. Meanwhile Gordie drifted up and down the line quietly checking on everyone, taking the pulse of the group. This was done in a very unobtrusive way. He would move alongside, exchange a word or two and then move on. When he saw distress, he stayed to give support, to encourage and if he felt it was necessary, to suggest we stop and rest awhile.

Richard was the netkeeper at rear of the line. Anyone drifting back came into his embrace. No one could 'drop off the end' because he was the end. It was a difficult role he chose and a lonely one, but he was physically strong and very fit.

We walked in single file. The line was very elastic, stretching and contracting and stretching again and threatening to break. Yet we were learning to help each other, to reach out a hand to boost a companion over an obstacle, to trust another's strength. But we were not yet twelve walking as one. The intention was there but the catalyst that fires and bonds was not.

Day three dawned to sweeping rains. A wild storm passed through in the night to lash the trees and smash the tent flat. Those in the comfort and warmth of the hut were reluctant to rise and greet the day. I was very tempted to wait out the rains but felt we should not spend another night on this side of the river. We had crossed the Arahura River on a swingbridge to reach this hut and in doing so left the Peace Trail. I wanted to return to that trail. We were equipped for the rain, we were heading for another hut, it seemed an acceptable choice. I decided to go.

Perhaps if I'd been more open to the guidance from within, and other signs around me, I'd have snuggled down in a bunk and enjoyed a rest. It was so confusing for me in this space between the cultures.

Think on this. When I rose before dawn to light the trail fire in the forest, I crouched in heavy rain and strong winds. Was there a message in that? When I got the fire going and performed the ritual of the trail stones one fell from my wet hand and landed across the circle. Was there a message in that? When I looked to the hills the rain was sweeping across them to form a curtain. Was there a message in that? Riroriro, the trail bird had not sung that morning. Was there a message in that? Yes, there were messages in all those things but they were confusing or contradictory. I felt the call of the trail.

We bravely set off for the next hut. The rain fell steadily. This was to be one of the hardest days of my life and each step remains carved in memory. We rapidly climbed out the valley to join the high trail again. There were many side streams to cross but they were all manageable and we were moving as a very close group at good speed. I was really impressed and could see us reaching the next hut in a few hours.

Puke hadn't come to me that morning to speak of the next sacred rock. I only realised that when he appeared beside me and said...

'I can hear a drum beating. It's very loud. It goes - booom, booom, booom!'

'What kind of drum is it Puke?'

'It's made of wood - like a fence post hollowed out. Someone is beating it with another piece of wood. It's a long way off but it's very loud.'

I couldn't hear the drum but I knew Puke was sharing something that was very clear to him.

What did it mean? I didn't understand its message until it was too late to act on it. I went to a tall tree beside the trail and used the end of the tokotoko to beat a response into its trunk. A kind of 'message received' signal.

We pushed on. Rain continued to fall but now it was driven by a rising wind. I could see the Styx Saddle outlined a few minutes away. Once there the way ahead was easier and the ridge would provide better shelter. Then we encountered a side stream that was running too fast and too deep to cross. Downstream a little, Pete found a way over with the help of rocks and a fallen branch. People and packs were ferried across quickly without difficulty.

The Saddle beckoned. Within moments we came to the last stream that could keep us from the hut ahead. It was impossible to cross. We had to return to the hut we left that morning. The danger now was that the side streams behind us would rise too fast to allow us through. If that happened we would have to camp on the track. We had the tents to do this but there was very little room. It would be a wet, uncomfortable night.

The first obstacle on our retreat to the hut was the flooded stream we had just crossed. All went well with Pete as the pivot until Caroline reached out for his hand and lost her footing and spun into the churning waters. Somehow he held her even though his grip was initially only on four fingers. He jumped into the water and wedged his body behind the sturdy branch that was our bridge. Caroline was completely under the water. It thrust past her with such power a rooster's tail a metre high formed over her head. Within seconds Gordon, Pere and Petariki joined Pete to help take the strain. It took four of them several minutes to pull her upstream against the current and over the branch to safety. How Pete held her I'll never know. How the others could respond so quickly still amazes me. Caroline came within a hand's span of losing her life.

We immediately got her into dry clothes and moved her back down the track. Supporting her, keeping her moving, running warmth into her chilled body. After a few minutes we slowed and reassembled and moved cohesively. Now each side stream became a barrier. Sometimes the flooded streams could only be bridged with Pete setting himself in the centre of the flow. He put his back into the waters and angled his long staff out front as a third leg. He was the bridge that saw us through. Again and again his skills eased the way. Eventually we gained the shelter of the hut, badly shaken by the experience. Today the trail had taken on frightening dimensions and raised many questions.

We sat around the fire, dried and fed, and discussed the day. We considered going back. All kinds of doubts surfaced. This was good for we called up and faced our fears. Our first concern was for Caroline and Derek. She'd been through a terrifying experience. He had seen his daughter a moment away from being swept to her death.

Derek and I had been close friends for many years. Together we wrote, illustrated, designed and published our own books on the outdoors. At one level it was a business but in reality it was just fun. His mind has a clarity that few people I've met have come close to matching. He cut to the heart of an issue with startling truth. Such people are rare for there is mind and heart in tune within him.

We all waited on Caroline's words, wanting to know how she saw the trauma of the flooded stream. She had handled the retreat to the hut bravely, was positive, shared her fears and came to a decision. 'I want to go on. I want to finish the journey.' Her father supported her wish to complete the trail.

Everything had changed. The journey had taken on another dimension. The challenge of the trails was very real, and it was faced and accepted. The walkers stood taller, knew more about themselves and liked what they saw. Twelve now walked as one, aware of the dangers, determined to see it through and committed to meet the deepest needs of each other. Adversity had created bonds that knew no bounds.

As I lay on the bunk watching six of the party sitting astride a long stool giving each other a back massage, Puke's voice echoed in my mind...

'Booom. Booom. Booom went the drum!'

Out of that beat came the answer. Words spoken weeks ago surfaced to strike me with jolting force...

'A drum will beat out the footsteps at dawn and as the Sun goes down.'

I had forgotten the drum would only sound twice a day. When it beat just before noon it was a warning, a desperate attempt to alert us to the danger ahead. I'd missed it.

Day four dawned with clear skies. We left early and found the streams had returned to normal levels overnight. The mood was subdued, but determined, as we closed up and made excellent time. I was so pleased when I rounded a bend to find the Styx Saddle revealed in all its power. Pausing to enjoy the Sun and take in the wonder of it all, I was delighted to hear the harsh cry of a kea. It was circling high above the pass.

Then my mind shifted and spun into another space to be filled by the voice of one of the elders. I remembered something. He was reciting a prophecy, seeding it deep within me late in the night. I was so tired it slipped into some secret place without resistance and beyond memory. Those sessions were weeks ago but the words began to ripple through me like a pulse of light...

'Pause as you come to the opening to the pass. If it is a true trail, the ancestors will send a kea to circle above and call to you, and another to fly low to meet you.'

The kea still wheeled and cried high above the pass. Then swift movement drew my eyes down to the treetops. A second bird flew low out of the pass at tremendous speed. I was transfixed. Its flight was like an arrow, straight and true. My first thought was, 'This can't be a kea,' but as it swept by its cry proved me wrong. A great wellspring of joy rose within me. I stood there and wept and, when the others arrived, found I couldn't really explain the wonder of that moment. The flight of the kea, the ground hawks of the mountains, said, 'You walk a true trail.'

We came to the stream that had nearly claimed Caroline's life. We gave thanks for her return to us, for yesterday's safe retreat to the hut and for the courage to complete the journey.

Song and laughter were our companions as we moved on to find the next sacred doorway. We broke out of the treeline to enjoy the Sun and spectacular views of the Arahura River far below.

Two hours later I was surprised to find Pere beside me. He looked concerned and said...

> 'Uncle Barry, my hands are tingling and I think I understand what that means. I must apologise. When you asked if I had information about the trails, I was sure I didn't know anything. But now I am beginning to remember something.'

> 'Do you think you can help me find the next doorway?' I asked with some relief because Puke had not come forward at all.

> 'Yes. I now remember being kept awake very late. Then, as I was drifting in and out of sleep, I was told things that are only now coming back to me. When my hands tingle it is a sign that we are close to the rock. I will know it when I see it.'

Pere stayed with me and a little later pointed to the doorway. It matched the description given. We waited for the others to gather at the rock to prepare for the lifting of the tapu. Puke was the first to arrive and he was upset and vocal...

'That's not the rock!' he exclaimed. 'It's just back there.' I went with him to the rock he felt was the right one.

This was difficult. 'Puke, that's a very special rock, one of great power,' I said, 'I don't understand why it is calling to you so strongly. It is not the one we seek this time.'

Puke had indeed tuned into a special rock. It was not part of our journey but was clearly part of his. So Puke stayed with it for a long time.

This was the last time Puke used his 'sight' to find the doorways. I wondered if he had come to a boundary of some kind and his work was done. He had switched to another wavelength when Pere had switched on. The elegance of so much that was happening almost overwhelmed me at times.

We were now above the treeline. Alpine grasses and low bushes were our companions. Before us stretched the last adventure on the trail this day. A long swingbridge spanned a deep gorge. One by one we crossed it, swaying over the drop into the churning waters far below. Some hurried over to reach firm ground. Others stopped in the middle to feed on the majesty of the surrounding snow covered peaks, the brilliant blue waters beneath, the sentinal rocks so sheer and powerful and the breath-stopping thrill of hanging in space on strands of wire.

We came to the hut well before sunset. Here the earth oozed water and swamp grasses flourished in the dips and hollows. It was difficult to pitch a tent so all twelve crammed into a hut designed for six. Yet home was never so comfortable and cosy.

The Moon brought a beautiful light to the mountains and the stars beckoned. Pere invited us outside to show how his ancestors used star markers to locate the pass ahead. I had been this way before and knew the break in the surrounding peaks that signalled the way through. He was new to this trail. So it was very satisfying to see his hand reach out to a sequence of stars, and make the intersections, and descend to cut the line to the pass. Once again the old lore of the trails was being carried into the next generation. Opening the trail opened the mind and freed the spirit to soar the heights again. Tomorrow we would walk there.

Day five dawned with clouds building in the west. We intended to leave early to keep ahead of the breaking weather. Every step and stumble along the trail brought us to this moment. Before us stood the Main Divide of the Southern Alps. Today we would walk across the shoulders of ancestors of great mana, brave ones remembered in stone and honoured for their courage and wisdom. We travelled in the strength of the Old Ones who had gone before us and the prayers of elders who fasted each day to open the way. They were all very close.

My thoughts were often of home, of Barbara who did so much, with such quiet efficiency, to help in the preparations. Yet we parted at the track head without embrace or a word of farewell. I was so immersed in gathering the party together, urging this one and that one to complete the last minute packing of bits and pieces that we were five minutes down the track before I realised what had happened. I wanted to stop, to run back, to put it right, but I couldn't. We were committed and I couldn't walk back over my footsteps.

I learnt much from that parting. One Kaumatua often said, 'No fancy goodbyes. Just go.' Leave taking was a real ritual with me, an important part of friendship, something to be done thoughtfully. 'Just going,' was very hard for me. By way of explanation I'd been told 'Goodbye closes the door,' but that hadn't touched anything real within me. This abrupt broken departure certainly did. For the next few hours I felt at a loss, saddened, and very close to Barbara. Then it hit me. She seemed to be alongside. It was a beautiful moment and a very deep realisation, 'Goodbye does somehow close the door.' The power is in the thought. If we leave the space others may remain close by to share our journey if they wish.

Jo had something exciting to tell us that morning. She said...

'We had a visit in the night. Everyone else seemed to be asleep. I was wide awake, light was still escaping from the firebox so it wasn't very late. The face of an elder appeared before me, then he moved on to look at each of you.'

Today was so important. I sat aside to think about the trail ahead, to create a quiet space, room for the wairua to move. Jo's story turned through my mind like a key turning in a lock to open a door. A name found voice. 'Raureka.' Then other words emerged, words buried deep in earlier days, words of caution...

'If the face of a woman appears to anyone in the party as you approach the pass you must stop immediately. Heed her warning. She is Raureka, the Keeper of the Trail.'

Raureka was born of the mountain people and those who walked with the stone. That was many centuries ago in the earlier days of the Nation. She was trained in the lore of the trails and called to serve the people on the passes. Her life was dedicated to guiding the stone carriers through the wilderness. She travelled this trail with her dogs, her only companions on some lonely journeys.

Sometimes the elders sent her to the passes to meet a party from the east to bring them safely to the waters of the western shores. At other times she guided twelve from the villages of Hokitika, Arahura or Pa Roa to the pass. There she gave them into the hands of another who led them safely through the eastern trails.

Storms created the greatest hazards in the mountains. They brought the snows to the heights and released the heavy rains that give birth to the flood-tides that made the rivers uncrossable. The trails were only open in the warmer months.

The day came when Raureka was sent into the mountains late in the summer to await a party journeying from the east. She arrived at the given time on the right quarter of the Moon and camped in the pass with her dogs. She looked east each day, sweeping the long valley below with keen eyes, anxious to gather in those she would guide westwards and concerned to be out of the mountains before the snows came.

Dawn followed dawn. No one arrived. Raureka's supply of smoked eel, so favoured by the mountain people, was finished. Was she now free to return to her home in the west? No! She decided to stay, to be there if the party arrived, to honour the way of the trail.

The snows fell heavily that night. Dawn revealed the ancestors standing tall and strong, wearing their beautiful korowai huka, their cloaks of snow. The mountains were silent.

In the springtime, when the yellow flowers of kowhai marked the trails again, the people found Raureka. She was still waiting for the party to appear from the east. Her bones rested there, testimony to service, and beside them the bones of her companions who stayed by her side.

The spirit of Raureka still travels the trail to guide those who walk in peace. And the bark of her faithful dogs echoes through the valleys in the night. We heard them. They were ever present.

When we formed the circle for the karakia I put Raureka there, saying...

> 'Should you see the face of a woman in the mist or the clouds, or strongly in your mind as we climb the pass, I want you to tell us.
>
> Don't hesitate. Trust what you see. Speak out.'

The previous evening we discussed how to get Petariki, the strong Whale, over the pass. Until now we had travelled beside the waters of a great river and the spirit of the whale found a trail there. Today we would leave the river and climb above rocky bluffs and over open, rock-strewn lands foreign to the giant keepers of the sea trails.

Gordon came up with the answer. He was of the waters, walked with the spirit of the ancestors and worked as a water scientist. If there was no water he would carry it. If the whale needed to be guided over foreign terrain he would guide it through by the hand. Petariki said he was very happy with this. At last we were ready to depart.

There was one sacred door to open before the final ascent to the pass. It was far from the trail of today and added more time to the journey. However, there were rewards for the extra effort. As we approached the rock we came upon a family of blue ducks in a beautiful pool. These gentle creatures of the fast mountain streams have no fear of humans. Perhaps that is why they are now so few.

We stand beneath towering cliffs. It is as if the heart of the mountain is revealed. Awesome is the only word that fits this place. The doorway is before us, strong, enduring and above it soars walls of stone. My focus shifts as I gaze on them, and the angles join and reform, and with startling clarity the huge head of an ancestor appears. It is magnificent, chiefly, wise and speaks of many worlds, many times and many peoples. Gordon sees other images and we share his excitement when the dogs of Raureka emerge to take their place in the interplay of shadow and light.

We return to our packs in the valley to find kea amusing themselves shredding sleeping mats strapped to the sides. Pete sat on the grass and put some butter on his staff. The kea circled, then one landed nearby, hopped about in their cheeky, comical way and suddenly flew to the top of the staff. This adventurer enjoyed the butter and even agreed to take some gently from Pete's finger with its wickedly hooked beak. This visit by the ground hawks of the trail brought great mana to the journey.

The way was open to the pass. Some say these last hours of steady, rhythmical climbing are a meditation. It is wearying and the mind does go within. Yet the land speaks and calls the spirit to fly free, to reach out to the vast horizons that open up. Only those who make the journey know the depth of this.

We broke through to the final slopes, looked back upon the immensity of the Arahura valley and its upper gorges for the last time, and embraced snow covered peaks that took our breath away. And then I saw the whale.

Across the narrows of the final gorge was a wide scree slope that skirted the highest mountain in view. It was like a huge grey canvas and leaping across it was a huge white whale with its mouth open. It was laughing. There was only one patch of snow on the scree and it had been shaped with great artistry to become a whale.

My first question to the Kaumatua of the trails when we arrived home was...

'How did the elders put the whale there?'

'They didn't. You did,' was his reply.

Thus was Petariki made welcome amidst the snow. He and Gordon had walked the arid heights together. Now the Whale People were truly of this trail. And it didn't stop there, for when I had time to reflect on this aspect of the journey, I realised if a whale could make it over the pass the trail was now open to everyone. A huge change had been 'accidentally' introduced. In the past this trail was the domain of very few. The Mountain People, who came from a homeland bounded by peaks and visited by snows were at home here. They ensured the route was maintained, shelters were ready, food stocks in place and the stone was carried through each year. The Stone People who walked with the spirit of the pounamu and carved it for the Nation were also free to move in these alpine lands. Similarly there were no borders to the realms of the Water People. None may challenge the trails chosen by water.

The Garden People did not walk here. The Whale People, the Dolphin People, the Tree People and many others were foreign to these slopes. That lore served the Nation well in other times and was to be honoured and respected. Today the dream was being made anew, the circle was being drawn again to open the way for all young people to explore new horizons. The prayers of the elders, the strength of Petariki, the support of the twelve, the hand of Gordon and my 'mistake' made that possible.

Soon after sighting the whale we discovered snow covered the path. This was part of the Kuia's dream. Yesterday she had shared her yearning for the snow to be there to honour the walk. I remembered the words spoken by an elder before leaving...

> 'It will be a moment of great rejoicing if your trail crosses the snow. But heed this well. Do not depart from the path to seek it.'

We formed our circle in the snow and said karakia. We gave thanks for all the blessings of this day. We held the snow in our hands until we felt its coldness bite deep. We were strong and alive. We moved on to stand beside the sacred lake that fills the summit of the pass. That day it was a remarkable sight with the light dancing over the waters and little icebergs floating away from a huge wall of drifted snow that had gathered in the past winter. This is how Ngahue, Poutini and Rakaihautu saw it so long ago. Here the stone carriers rested before journeying on. Here Raureka gave her life as she waited for the people to arrive from the east.

We took food then moved on quickly as heavy clouds gathered behind us in the west. It was important to leave before the weather broke. I had spoken to none of the party about the route off the pass. I just took them there and let them find within themselves the courage to descend.

The pass we know as Browning is a great challenge. It's hard to convey how impossible that descent appears to those who are new to the mountains. Everything just drops away to fall thousands of feet to a distant ribbon of water. The mind says, 'I can't go down there. No one can go down there.' And it's not just a mind thing, the stomach tumbles to support those words. It's all too much.

No one spoke their anxieties aloud. Their faces said it all but there wasn't a single query. Nothing. They would simply get on and do it.

Pete, Gordon and I scouted ahead to find a route off the top. We danced down the slopes, revelling in the drama of those alpine peaks, exhilarated by the huge scale of this world. We were at home here. Free as in no other place.

We secured a guide rope and closed the group up and began the climb down. In the beginning it was simply terrifying for some of the party, but they made jokes about their ability to become 'starfish' and attach themselves to the rocks when parked up and waiting for others to move. Then confidence grew, the drop off became manageable, and we moved steadily down towards the river far below. When we broke through to the scree slope the more experienced began to run it with whoops of joy. Then others gave it a try and an exuberant mountain madness swept us down to where the trail waited.

An hour later we reached our camp for the night. Our message to the elders at day's end was, 'The whale has crossed the mountain.'

By the light of the camp fire I reflected on the journey. What was I learning? Some of the young ones were polishing their pounamu, using natural oil from their bodies to bring out its beauty. We polish the stone, the trail polishes us. It was indeed a trail of the spirit. As we walked the mountains we travelled deeper and deeper into ourselves.

Day six arrived and the rain clouds continued to stay in the west. A giant hand held them at bay and stilled the flood-tides. Now only two crossings of the Wilberforce, the great river swept by the winds, stood between us and a safe end to the trail. It has claimed many lives. We were all very tired now and footsore. However, we walked for each other, sharing our strengths. In the final two days we traversed wide grassy river flats bathed in sunshine with warm norwest winds at our backs. We walked in pairs, hand in hand. There were still three doorways to open.

Pere helped us find the next one. As we entered the deep valley that branched off the Wilberforce River, he stopped and shared a vision that was before him. He saw the doorway and standing before it was a chief wearing a fine cloak of feathers to greet us. Soon after we came to that place. A rainbow played beside the high waterfall on the skyline behind the sacred rock. We were indeed welcome.

Here I found the eleven red trail stones I needed at the end of the journey. I was told they would await me on the way but nothing more. The search for these stones had been with me each day. Their weight in my pocket was very reassuring. It was a relaxing time. We crossed the river without difficulty and found a place to camp under the trees. We thought there was little food left, but with the help of bits and pieces from here and there, and a major contribution from Petariki, we created a meal to remember. We shared our stories of the trail around the fire.

Day seven began hours before the summer dawn. It was a long walk out and the families would be waiting. The sixth doorway was close to our line of travel and we came to it as the first light of the sun reached into the valley. Our songs grew ever stronger to honour those who came this way before us. Weary to the bone, but finding resources never dreamt of, we moved on knowing the last doorway was still some hours away.

We came to the musterers' hut. It was off our direct route but for some reason I changed direction. That was meant to be. We entered and our hearts leapt high. The table was beautifully set with bowls of bananas, oranges, and apples, plates of fresh bread, butter, jam and biscuits, cakes and fruit juices. Everything we had been dreaming of over the last hot and dusty days.

A Kaumatua had walked in with my youngest son Rod, and Tama, a friend, to prepare this wonderful surprise. They will never fully understand what that meant to us.

With two hours remaining to complete the trail we set off. We rested often and spent a long time in one very special place to honour the memory of an old man who died there many generations ago. He was with a trail party, moving late in the season, that was caught in a snow storm. He stopped here, sat quietly on the ground and said...

> 'My journey is over. Yours still stretches before you. Leave me now. Return for my bones when the snows have gone from the mountains and the kowhai blooms.'

There were others who gave their lives to serve the stone on this trail. It asks much and gives much in return.

Leaving our packs by the track we went to find the last of the sacred rocks, the seventh doorway. The heat of the day and the weariness of the last three days failed to slow our pace now. This was a special moment, for the rock not only honoured an ancestor of great mana, but was the last. Here we closed the trail on our journey. The way was made easy for us. As we moved up the wide river bed we saw here and there stones that did not rest easily. None were set in the form of cairns but there were subtle realignments that pointed the way. A trail maker had used ancient markings to guide us quickly to the oldest of the doors.

I have many wonderful memories of that rock. Jo sang the African 'click' song with such power I felt it cross the mountains and span the oceans of the world to return and say, 'We are one, brothers and sisters, children of the Earth. It is time to honour the best in all of us.'

So much ancient wisdom bound within stone. The grandmother of the sacred doorways seemed to say...

'Here the trail begins and here it ends. Here time folds over time. Here the stars touch the earth. Here young people find the dream. Here all the world joins as one.'

Returning to our packs we continued towards a low saddle as a close group. Then on the horizon a figure stood against the sky, moved and the families gathered. They could not come to meet us. We had to come to them. The journey was nearly over.

A marae had been created at the Harper village. We entered through a gateway of two beautiful pieces of pounamu to be welcomed in the old way. We responded to their words and sang our trail songs. Richard played the story of the journey on his koauau, a wooden flute, with all his wonderful touch. Each of the walkers received from my hand a red stone for the journey made and the life trails that opened before them. It was done.

When does this story end? Perhaps the answer is, 'Now and never'. The trail still weaves its way into my life. It is a watershed. I had walked the realms of magic and felt the excitement of it deep within me. I had reached beyond myself and dreamed new dreams. It was both exhilarating and frightening. I needed a map to guide me through this new land.

Ash gathered on the trail was taken to Pani Manawatu. He held it before him. When it ignited and burned with a bright blue flame he said...

'It is good. Everything was done with love.'

I remembered how each day on the trail we mistakenly took the stance of warriors to walk the Peace Trail. Did that herald a new way? Was it now the age of the peaceful warriors? Those who walk with courage to respect the earth and all within it and beyond; those whose only weapons are gentleness and love. Other words found voice...

'Centuries ago...Tohunga with the power of prophesy proclaimed the day would come when the stars would align in a very special way. When that came to pass two things would follow.... the most sacred of knowledge would be shared with everyone...and the people of peace would stand and walk tall again...'

There was no one map for this journey. I was sailing uncharted waters that reached into the world of ancestors in Europe, Africa, Asia, the Americas, the world of Waitaha in the Pacific and the world of the spirit. I was in the world and between worlds. All I had to guide me was a compass that said, 'Follow your heart. Do everything with love.'

Where does the circle begin?
Where does the story end?
Now and never.

TIME AND TIDE

'Go back on to the trails... Be humble, listen to the land, listen to those who will guide you through the land... Write what you learn and hear in peace and love.'

Pani Manawatu's words were strong markers for my journey with 'Song of Waitaha'. We had returned to the ancient trails, lifted the tapu and carried the stone to clear the way for the sacred knowledge to be written. It was time to learn to walk the path of the knowledge.

We needed very practical help to get the work started. Back in October of 1988 the Minister of Internal Affairs was approached to approve the attachment of three of the team to his department for twenty months. That request got lost somewhere in the political labyrinth but the book was approved in December as an official 1990 Commemorative Celebration project.

In late January, with the education year about to commence, I was concerned about staffing the work. Ultimately it would require five people to carry the kaupapa, the dedicated task, to completion. I approach Pani Manawatu for advice and out of our discussions came a one page letter written in his name and addressed to the Prime Minister, David Lange.

Within a week I was urgently called to the office of the principal of the Teachers College. He was talking to the head of personnel in the Department of Education. When I took the phone a rather incredulous official on the other end said...

'Mr. Brailsford, I have in front of me a memo from the Prime Minister. It is unlike any I have received before. It is a small piece of paper attached to your letter, and simply says...

Make it happen, do it now, get the funds from Vote Education.'

This meant three of us would be freed for twenty months to work on the book from May 1989. The waka was moving but I had much to learn before I'd be able to navigate it. At the outset I thought I was reasonably well equipped to do so as I had already written 'The Tattooed Land' and 'Greenstone Trails'. Yet within a short time I began to realise I really knew very little about the history that was now being revealed.

This was bad enough for the part of me that was the historian and archaeologist. There was more. Initially I thought I was to be a writer. That ancient knowledge would be given into my care and I would sit down and do my stuff on the computer. The need to open the Peace Trail to begin the book blew that idea away. My focus had been on gathering, processing and writing information. That had changed. It was clear the 'way and when' of things was paramount.

As facilitator of the team I saw myself as a planner and administrator who would push the job through. After many months of experiencing the agony of schedules that fell apart, journeys that stretched far beyond my time allocations, hours, even days spent waiting for something to happen, I began to get the message. This wasn't the way. Everything was adrift and I wondered if I was either in the wrong waka or the wrong ocean. In reality I was in the wrong space. I was driven by time instead of seeing the place of timing, and focused on the destination instead of the journey.

None of this was taught to me by explicit instruction. That was not the way. I was not allowed a teacher. The invocation to, 'Listen to those who will guide you through the land,' was filled with subtlety. I began to understand no one was going to say directly to me, 'Do this' or 'Do that'. I had to open my head, heart, eyes, ears and every aspect my being to 'the way', whatever that was and whatever that meant.

Somehow learning seeped into me by a process of osmosis as I became 'deprogrammed'. Gradually I began to see some of the useful 'baggage' I carried through childhood, school days, teaching career and executive work was useless on this trail. I was great at getting things done quickly. Thought was swiftly followed by action that cut through non-essentials and got to the heart of problems. I moved rapidly on many fronts, often having several major projects going forward at the same time. I'd caught the modern disease of doing many things at one time, juggling my attention between this and that and being very busy.

'Do one thing at a time' was my first great lesson. This sounds very simple, and it is, but there is deep wisdom in its practice. Having been asked to make several 300 kilometre trips to the West Coast quite close together, I realised each journey was for one task alone. Looking back I saw we could have done everything the first time and still had room for other work as well. So I asked myself some searching questions and came up with the standard answers - this kind of thing was 'inefficient', 'wasted valuable time' and 'would drive an accountant mad'.

However, when I searched below the surface of this apparent inefficiency I began to see good reasons for 'doing one thing at a time'. It honoured each task as special, gave it mana and ensured it was done well in every dimension. A trip to the West Coast to obtain pounamu in 1989 involved a day's travel. If that was the only 'take' or task, there was time for karakia to begin and end the trip, time to spend with those who gathered the stone and time for them to tell the story of the stone. Space existed for the 'unexpected' to bring additional riches to the journey - for the wairua to move, for the spirit to be present. Only then was the integrity of the task complete.

Centuries ago the pounamu carried over the Peace Trail often took several years to reach the east coast. By design it didn't travel all the way in one summer season. It was left to feel the touch of snow and the alpine rains. It waited in the foothills until the stone carriers called it home. It was honoured at every step, for the people answered a higher call than that of 'efficiency' and 'time wasting'. I liked that sense of the tides of time - a way of being and moving that harboured respect and bonded everything to the land itself.

Pounamu is a very hard stone for it is nephrite, a member of the jade family. Today it is cut with diamond saws. Its strength is born of the turmoil and travail of the shaping of the land itself over hundreds of millions of years. The parent material, the mother of pounamu, is sometimes soft enough to be scored by a finger nail. However, when it is caught within the great fault lines of the Southern Alps and subjected to enormous grinding and pressure the crystals realign and interlock to create a very tough stone.

The ancestors cut and polished pounamu with other stone. Greywacke spawls struck from large beach stones were used, and sandstone, at the polishing stage. It was difficult, skillful work, but pounamu adzes and amulets could be completed in a few months. However, some pieces which were very special, took several centuries to be finished. I would like to share the story of the making of such a treasure.

A young man born to the stone rises to greet the sun. It is a special day for he has dreamed a stone and heard it calling from the river. He is of the Stone People and such a vision is a matter for great rejoicing.

The way is opened with karakia and he journeys to the Arahura River to answer the call and lift the pounamu from the waters. It is raining heavily. He moves urgently to free it from the rising waters that might sweep it into the deeps. He names this wondrous stone and becomes its keeper.

The day arrives when he begins to carve the stone and free the image he sees within. He moves with great respect for his life is dedicated to cutting into the depths of stone without destroying its spirit. After many days he has completed the first cut. Then it is put aside in a special place of caring and taken to the waters from time to time. He will do no more in his lifetime. The next cut will fall to his son or even his grandson. They in turn will share the journey of the stone.

Over many generations the adze within that stone slowly emerges as each carver leaves his mark. Eventually it is ready to carve wood. The cutting edge is sharp and true but it is still not finished. There is much to do before it is fully shaped and polished. Meanwhile, it serves the people well year after year, carving waka to sail to distant shores and ancestral posts for the great meeting house.

Another born to the line receives the adze and knows it is time to finish the shaping begun so long ago. It is completed at last and is truly a beautiful taonga. Never again will this adze be hefted high to bite deep into the wood. Its work is done. It is a treasure beyond price, touched by the spirit of all who gave their skill and nurture to the stone and held it close over so many years. It holds great mana and its journey of inspiration and power has just begun.

There is an amazing sense of the continuity of life in the creation of this taonga. The gifting from generation to generation, the letting go, the sharing of the joy of its making and the trust that it will one day be completed. We remember here another age, another tide, another trail and a very different sense of time and purpose.

I was between cultures, learning about timing, letting go, listening to the land and listening to my heart. I was reprogramming. I was a partly formed adze emerging from ancient stone.

There were so many old ways to put aside. Time watching, the constant need to squeeze task after task into boxes of 'accomplishments', things done and put aside, things finished according to the timetable. Yet done and finished in isolation. Often completely divorced from other considerations. Honouring the call to 'Do one thing at a time', helped me move beyond that.

I was discovering the seasons of life. There were hundreds of seasons and through them ran many tides. There was great joy in moving to their rhythms.

FINDING THE VOICES OF THE ANCESTORS

'I heard the voices of the old ones joined with the music of the land.'

This morning I was upset about what I have been writing in these pages. The words were flowing as never before but it was becoming painful to the point of tears. Sometimes I simply felt overwhelmed. Then my own words returned, 'I am writing this book to heal myself.' I am returning to the hurt and confusion to be freed of it, to call out the pain. That is the journey I chose at the outset. So be it. Continue.

Then another concern stood before me. When I set out to share my journey with 'Song of Waitaha' I wanted to embrace the adventure of it all, the excitement and the wonder. I knew this would bring us into things magical and mystical, but I didn't realise it would happen so often.

I seem to be constantly writing of wonderful 'coincidences' that put people and events into the 'right place at the right time', compassionate 'mistakes' that bring great changes to our lives and happy 'accidents' that open doors where we think none exist. And when that's not happening I'm describing mind linking to mind, time folding over itself to bring now and tomorrow together, seeing ahead to map places as yet unvisited and other glimpses of another reality.

'This is just too much,' was my reaction. 'People will think I'm crazy, there's too much magic.' Then I stopped and asked myself...

'Am I making all this up? No!

Can I tell the stories with integrity and hide the magic? No!

Then what's the problem?'

The voice of Kaylynn Two Trees of the Lakota Nation and a beautiful friend, filled my mind. When last we met she said...

'We need to accept the magic as normal. Not to just go Wow! and get swept away and lost in it.

The magic is there all the time. It's always been there but most of us have carefully unlearned it. Society feels uncomfortable with things beyond science as we know it.

The magic is simply the way. Expect it, accept it, enjoy it, say, 'Thank you' and get on with the journey.'

So that crisis of confidence passed and I moved on to answer questions people bring to the book. When asked...

'How was 'Song of Waitaha' written?' I am often tempted to reply, 'At 4.00 o'clock in the morning on the Moon.'

That's the truth of how the work was done but it needs explanation. Yes, I did begin writing at 4.00 o'clock, an unusual hour for me, and it happened this way. In the weeks before we set off to open the Peace Trail in 1988, I was very busy organising for the journey, outfitting the walkers with packs and clothes, setting up transport to and from the trail, seeing to the food and tents, plus keeping my work going at the Teachers College. Somewhere in there I needed to find a space for the most demanding part of all, learning the trail lore. How could I find a quiet time free of interruption to learn the karakia? It had to be word perfect and that didn't come easy to me. It was a problem.

Suddenly I began to wake at four o'clock every morning. This was not to answer the call of my alarm clock or by any conscious design. My normal waking time was about seven. This was definitely abnormal, but I was so wide awake at four it was impossible to settle back to sleep so I used the time to study the karakia and the lore. When I mentioned this early waking to an elder he simply smiled and said...

'That's a wonderful time for learning. It's the wairua time, the time of the spirit.'

Although rather naive at that stage I suspected someone had 'tampered' with my internal clock. It was indeed a wonderful time to work, so when the writing began to fill my life I happily answered the early call and entered the 'wairua time'.

Those early hours between four and eight were very special, timeless even, with hours seeming like minutes. The moment I woke I knew what I was going to write about, which of the baskets of knowledge I was going to open, everything.

The sacred knowledge has been kept within the Whare Wananga, a highly disciplined school of learning, for thousands of years. It is both universal and particular. Universal in that the spirit of it, the core understandings bound together as the lore, are common to many indigenous peoples. I could sit with Hawaiian, Hopi, Cherokee, Chippewa or Crow elders and it was the same as sitting with Waitaha. It is particular because every story and understanding is tied to a place, to the land, to the waters or the stars. Knowledge was 'recorded' in the land for all time.

The Tohunga, the wisdomkeepers, were trained from birth to carry the knowledge and keep it safe. Over a lifetime they learned countless songs and prayers that carried the knowledge. In accessing it, recalling it and giving it out to the world, they honoured the land, the Earth Mother, the waters, the Sky Father, the stars, the universe and the source of all. The knowledge was received in the sacred places, not sitting in a lounge. We sometimes travelled deep into the mountains to sleep beneath a rock to wait to hear the words, or to a wild stretch of coastline or a lake. The knowledge and the land are one. When we bulldoze and blast 'sacred places' we destroy far more than we know.

Those who walk with the knowledge are few now. The Whare Wananga, the most ancient and sacred house of learning, 'died' in distant lands. When the Maori Battalion was formed to fight in the Second World War, the elders sent Tohunga with the young men, to nurture the spirit. This battalion took horrendous casualties and the wisdomkeepers, being called to the most dangerous places, died in great numbers in those foreign fields. And their bones still cry out to return to their families, to the sacred places and to the spirit of this land.

Born of the stars. These words fill my mind when I think of the wonder of those who carried the wisdom down the generations. They were indeed 'born of the stars' for only those whose birthing aligned with special stars, were called by the people to begin the journey. Few of the boys and girls who set out on that trail reached the doors of the school of learning and passed within. Only those who learned to walk with gentleness, who honoured the land and the ancestors, and had the mind and heart to carry the knowledge finished the journey.

Today the feats of memory achieved by the wisdomkeepers seem impossible, but that's because we underestimate the potential of the mind. People are often incredulous when I say the old ones memorised, word perfect, the songs that held the lore. I have heard the songs, the chants that take hours to deliver, and seen how the young can be taught to learn them.

At the beginning of the journey to open the Peace Trail, Pere denied all knowledge of the doorways along the way. Yet at the right time it was there, because he suddenly 'remembered' everything we needed to know about the next sacred rock. Pere was 'given' that knowledge late in the night when he was very tired and 'open' to receiving it. He didn't know what was set deep within his mind until something on the trail 'triggered' his memory and it tumbled out. This was but one of the many ways the knowledge was implanted.

During the Whare Wananga held in the north in 1990, I got only 6 hours sleep in four days. Whenever I tried to get away to catch up on lost sleep I was gathered in by someone and denied the opportunity. Later I was told the elders came at the end of that long 'awakening' and sang knowledge into me. I was unaware of that happening but when I returned home and began to write again I was making huge connections within the knowledge already given to me. This was very exciting. I was seeing the ancient world and its wisdom with amazing insight. Even more extraordinary was the new knowledge that jumped to the fore from time to time.

Ultimately the integrity of the knowledge depended on living it. It was the survival blueprint for the Nation - weather forecasting, gardening guidance, fishing lore, stone working techniques, shipbuilding designs, star observations, tide tables - real information that allowed the people to prosper in a real world.

Occasionally I'm asked, 'Who are the wisdomkeepers. Are we allowed to know their names?' They are few now and remain hidden, known only to those who are close to them. That is the way.

'How did you record the information given by the elders?' This question often surfaces when I tell stories about the book. Well, in the beginning I tried to tape it but that was disastrous. The machine malfunctioned, the technology got in the way of the words, it just didn't work. So in the end I sat and drew pictures as the knowledge was revealed and added a word here and there. Mainly I listened and let my mind open to wide horizons and depended on memory to hold the lore. When I returned from the sacred places I took my crumpled drawings out of my pack and sat for hours making the little pictures into bigger pictures, filling in detail, colouring them like a child, enjoying the thrill of it all.

It's important to understand nothing was given without me asking a question. It wasn't a matter of sitting beside a rock and asking the wisdomkeeper, 'Tell me about the journeys of Rakaihautu?', then listening to the complete story in twenty chapters. No, the questions had to be particular. 'What did Rakaihautu look like - the colour of his hair, his eyes, his height, and so on?'

The answers usually came after a long delay. It was like waiting for a tape recorder to wind on to the correct place. Of course that's very much what was happening. A song was being run through the mind, and access was being sought to a certain verse, and within that verse to particular words. The detail that was offered was staggering. It was possible to hear of the voyages of the ancestors on a day by day basis as if reading a ship's log. The names of the crew of 175 on the 'founding' waka that sailed 67 generations ago were all available. Also the plans for building the canoe, the dimensions of each crew space, the length of the sail and its shape, and the song charts and carved maps for the journey. It was like this with everything.

For me the most daunting part of the whole procedure was that 'Song of Waitaha' could only reach as far as my mind could travel. Its boundaries and its depths were 'limited' not by the knowledge available but by my understanding of the questions to ask, by my vision.

There was a problem here. From time to time I spun into the 'Why me?' space and railed at the universe, and anyone who would listen to my cry...

'I'm not trained for this, I'm out of my depth, someone else please take the responsibility.'

This inevitably led to the question, 'Who am I?' It in turn was followed by, 'What's my role?' So after the journey over the Peace Trail I said to myself, 'I am the Pae Arahi, the Trail Maker.' There was truth in that role for I had led the twelve and I was opening many other trails by writing the sacred knowledge for the first time.

However, when I took this to a Kaumatua he said, 'You are a Trail Maker, but there is more.' That wasn't very satisfactory, I wanted one label to hold on to, a box to fit into. Then I came to the conclusion I was a Story Teller and took that proposition to him. Once again I heard, 'Yes, you are indeed a Story Teller, but there is more.' This was one of those rare occasions when an elder showed impatience with me. Then I realised I had to live without a label, to see a world without a box to call my own, to be open to being all I could be.

If I settled for the roles of Trail Maker and Story Teller that would limit my horizons. So I am nothing and in that I am everything.

Only by moving into that space was I able to bring a big mind and heart to the work of 'Song of Waitaha'. There was another dimension to this. My initiation into the realms of the sacred knowledge set me on a path of risk and discovery. As I ventured into the unknown it was made clear to me I had to walk the trail of the spirit on my own. No one could advise me. I had to find my own way through the dark valleys and the high places. On those occasions when I felt very depressed and cried out for help, I was not answered. Fortunately I came to understand the kindness behind this compassionate neglect. I had to be my own person and walk my own trail without props, knowing my own strengths and growing into them.

A hand carried the sacred knowledge into this age - five people, five fingers worked on the book. This was the old way of moving with the strength and power to meet the challenge. Each finger had a very defined role. It was as if a circle surrounded my work and no one could step inside. It was like that for each of us. There was no advice, no directions, no instructions, just the awesome responsibility of getting it right.

When Derek, our art director and book designer, took his first photographs of a sacred place he did it in the knowledge that others had failed again and again. They shot the film but got nothing. One film crew even had their boat sink at its moorings before they got their cameras ashore. The elders were all smiles when Derek captured everything - images of majesty that spoke of ancient power in every print.

Derek's next mission was to photograph a sacred rock by the first light of the rising Sun. There was only one day of the year when this could be done. That was the easy bit. The real challenge was to capture the face of a woman on the rock's apparently smooth surface. He confided...

> 'I waited and waited to see that face appear. The dawn light struck the stone but no image emerged in the viewfinder. In the end I just took the photo and hoped.'

When the film was developed there it was - the extraordinary face of a beautiful woman. His work that dawn was rewarded by a double rainbow that arched over the rock to complete the moment. We often walked with the people of the rainbow.

I well remember Derek's struggle to design the marvellous tuatara engraving that protects the knowledge within 'Song of Waitaha'. He desperately wanted to see existing Waitaha carvings to understand the style but was denied access to them by the elders. The Kaumatua simply said...

> 'No one can speak to you of this. No existing carving can give you the answers you seek. You already know its shape and meaning. That knowledge is within you.'

Eventually Derek went to the West Coast to think about the tuatara. There he found the space to see it in all its power.

It was the same for the writing. No one would criticise my words or the way the stories were woven together. Sometimes that total freedom and absolute responsibility was a heavy load. Yet on reflection there could be no other way. We were asked to walk with the wairua of the old wisdom, to honour it as best we were able. To find truth within ourselves.

When I said to people I rose at four o'clock to write the book in the wairua time, some thought, 'Ah, he channelled the book. He went into a trance state and the words flowed through him.'

But that's not how it was. The knowledge came over many months, even years, and it followed paths opened by my questions. We would hear the lore of rainbows, wander into making the gardens and stay there for days, then explore weather forecasting and children's play. All the time I drew my pictures and stored them in a locked file and warmed them in my mind.

When I came to sit and write the story of an ancestor I called on everything in the picture bank. It wasn't channelled, it was painstakingly crafted with all the love I could bring to it. The mana of the ancestor was what I honoured.

This all sounds wonderful but in the beginning the writing did not go well. I didn't understand what was wrong, I just knew what I was writing did not work. This wasn't an archaeological text or the standard kind of history book. It called for something else - the poet, the writer and the spirit. Together they would bring the ancestors into this time and free the sacred knowledge to be shared. For some months the 'voices' did not come. The words were flat upon the page.

Each time the few, who walked close to the Histories, came to read my words they smiled and said 'How wonderful to hear the stories again.' Not a word of doubt or a word of criticism, just complete support. But I knew I was far from the trail I needed to travel. I was lost.

Then the time came when the words began to flow, the sentence patterns changed and 'clear voices' began to speak from within the tangled weave. My writing was beginning to reflect the light and shade that coloured the words of the elders on the marae. I heard the voices of the old ones joined with the music of the land itself. The sounds of the rivers, the cries of the birds, the strength of the tall trees, the enduring presence of stone and the warmth of the Sun gathered around the words. In the voices of the grandfathers and grandmothers the poet, the writer and the spirit became one. And here was the paradox - in becoming one they allowed a simple sentence to carry many levels of meaning. Truth was bound within truth, and within that truth, a deeper truth again was hidden. It was as it had always been.

I was excited by this writing. For fourteen days I stayed at home on the hill and wrote without acknowledging weekends or the world around me. When the readers came to sit with the 14,000 words I'd woven together in that time, they seemed to be taking forever over the task. I left to sit in another room, unable to bear the waiting. Time passed so slowly. I heard them enter in silence. There were none of the usual cries of 'It's wonderful, keep writing.' My head was down waiting for a word. They gathered around and I looked up to see they were crying. The Kaumatua said quietly, 'The wairua is there.' Poet, writer and spirit had joined.

What made that period of writing so different? What opened the door and brought such an excitement and creative power to the work? The Moon. I had worked on the right time of the Moon, from the first quarter through the full Moon to the last quarter. I had attuned myself to one of the greatest forces reaching into our lives from the heavens. The energy that makes the waters of the great oceans rise and fall, draws the sap up the trees and brings women to their seed tides each month is part of our being.

There are tides within each of us we sometimes sense but rarely honour. Something like eighty percent of our body is fluid. Our bodies, minds and emotions are far more aligned with the stars than we imagine. The Moon touches into our lives every moment of the day. How that affects us depends on the lunar cycle, the phases of the Moon. If we allow ourselves to perform the right work at the right time we release huge creative energies. That is what I had just experienced. Thereafter, I only wrote in the fourteen days of the bright Moon. The time of the dark Moon was for administration, planning, reflection and 'snuggling up' in bed, for this was the time of the lovers.

So 'Song of Waitaha' was written at 4.00 o'clock in the morning on the Moon. And there was a huge contentment in the writing. Time didn't exist, hours seemed like minutes. Sometimes I'd finish writing and get up from my computer and an amazing, exciting rush of energy would run through me. It was pure joy.

There was fun too. Sometimes I was surrounded by tricksters who took control of my computer. When I was describing measures taken to protect the fish breeding grounds from the ravenous squid I wrote...

'Arriving on the Bright Moon, they came in numbers we only kept at bay with a great net placed between the headlands.'

The moment I finished the last word the whole thing recomposed itself to look like this...

ArrivingontheBrightMoon,theycameinnumbersweonlykeptatbaywithagreatnetplacedbetweenthe

The words had joined to become a net that stretched across the page. Nothing like this had ever happened before. I carefully separated each word and they just as carefully rearranged themselves in a row without spaces. I was caught in a net and only got out of it with the help of a computer specialist. I was amused by this play on the words. Someone 'out there' had a wicked sense of humour.

On another occasion in an early draft I wrote...

'Tawhiri Matea, the God of Winds, strikes with an awesome, invisible hand to fell the tallest trees of the forest.'

Later that day as I printed out a copy, the ink began to fade at the word, 'Tawhiri' and everything became invisible until the word forest' gradually reappeared. The next line was normal. This was new behaviour for my printer, a trick it has never repeated. Obviously the joke wears thin the second time around.

The sacredness of the knowledge was something I lived with each day. Sometimes it all got a bit heavy. A little 'irreverence' had its place. It was important to 'lighten up'. The old ones on the stone trail of the Indian Nations said, 'Carry the heavy things lightly' and 'Dance the trail for you will only succeed if you travel with fun and laughter.' For years I'd joked about being a 'dancing leprechaun', so that fitted well.

When writing I put aside all thought of the significance of the work. It was necessary to enjoy the moment and not to think of what impact the words might have when they were published. If I hadn't done that I believe I'd have frozen at my computer, unable to type a word.

I became very close to the ancestors who walk the pages. For weeks at a time I journeyed with Maui, marvelled at his courage, his genius for innovation, his commitment to change and his vision for the people. I enjoyed the way he told stories against himself. I revelled in the wonderful voyages of Rakaihautu and his exploration of the mountain lands of Aotearoa. Ngahue and Poutini filled me with awe as they carried me into the realms of stone. Paparoa, Huaaki and Tira brought wonder to the lands of my birth. Wairau and Marotini taught me the ways of the gardeners and planted seeds of excitement. Each and every one filled my life.

'What you learn and hear, write in peace and love. ' That was not difficult.
I was telling the story of the people of peace and their world was love.

THE WAITAHA STORY

'If we are not gentle with life, the garden within us dies'

Perhaps it is time to write of the Nation of Waitaha. I'll not summarise 'Song of Waitaha', it's up to you to make the journey if you will. That's your voyage of discovery. My intent is to open other doors.

Waitaha was not one tribe, it was a Nation - a gathering of many tribes. The Nation was founded 67 generations ago by a waka with a crew of 175. There were equal numbers of men and women aboard and there were no children and no passengers. Waitaha always moved in the balance of men and women. On the waka were three very different races...

The white skinned people, with red or blonde hair, who were so pale they were freckled. They were a small people, navigators who knew the geometry of the stars.

The tall dark people, with black hair and brown eyes. Some would call them 'giants' for their bones indicate they were often well over six feet tall. They were wonderful gardeners who proved their skills by growing the frost tender kumara a thousand kilometres further south than in its South American homeland.

The olive skinned, dark haired, dark eyed people with a double fold over the eyelids. They were of the high mountains and the stone.

The founding of the Nation was neither haphazard nor accidental. The exploratory voyages of Maui, Tamatea Mai Tawhiti, and Ngahue and Poutini, charted the way for the outward journeys and the return home. With each voyage people were left in the new land to warm it. However it was only after 200 years of exploration that the founding waka made the long voyage to put the

Nation in place. Each member of that settlement capsule was very special, chosen for their place in the creation of the Nation.

The Nation of Waitaha eventually covered all the islands of Aotearoa and was committed to peace. Archaeologists find no weapons of war in the early sites of this land. Waitaha valued the varied skills of different peoples and honoured the idea of the old clans that carried particular ancient wisdoms forward into the future. Schools within the fire clan, the water clan, the tree clan, the stone clan, the star clan, the whale clan, the bird clan and many others were the universities of the sacred way. They preserved knowledge, recorded it in song and dedicated it to the needs of all within the Nation.

Great double-hulled waka sailed regularly to all coasts of the Nation. They carried industrial stone, seeds, food and songs forecasting the weather, the movement of the long tides, the stars and the spirit of the land and its waters. These vessels joined the Nation together and carried the brightest children of the tribes to schools of learning to keep the old lore safe for the unborn.

They knew the most precious gift in life was a healthy baby. Their waka returned again and again to the homeland and to other lands and brought new people to join the Nation. The crew that left Aotearoa was not the same crew that came home - often half were youths from other lands who sought adventure far beyond their homes. All were embraced for Waitaha understood strong children came of the mixing of blood.

For well over a thousand years the Nation lived in peace and grew to number more than two hundred tribes. Waitaha said...

> 'All born in this land are of this land. All who sleep beneath the mountains are of this land. All who choose to call this land home are of this land.'

The ancestors voyaged far to create the Nation. They believed there was a place for all and wonderful strength in diversity. They didn't create power structures to control the people or to give one section advantage over another. All had a place to stand tall. All who came in peace were welcomed. The bond that made them a Nation was commitment to Rongo Marae Roa, the Peace Maker. There were no institutions or buildings to honour that Guardian for there was no worship here, only reverence. The only place to hold the gentle spirit of Rongo Marae Roa was in the heart.

The Nation grew strong and the people were many. It did not collapse from within but fell when successive waves of warrior peoples arrived out of the Pacific in their waka of war.

The tragedy that befell the Moriori people of the Chatham Islands in the 1830s, is a documented account of the end of one of the tribes of the Nation. What happened to the Moriori echoes the fate of the other peoples of Waitaha centuries before.

When the warriors arrived from Taranaki on the sailing ship, they were but a few hundred. Denis Solomon, a Moriori elder, shared with me the way his ancestors faced the invaders. They gathered a thousand hunters, those dedicated to spill blood to feed the families by birding and fishing. Then the people came together to seek guidance from the ancestors in those days of dread and danger. And the words came...

'How we live is more important than how we die.'

With those words the Moriori firmly set their feet on the ancient trails of peace worn deep by their ancestors, and sealed their fate. The hunters were not unleashed to sweep the warriors into the sea. They extended the hand of friendship and when it was struck aside they went to their deaths without resisting the invaders. They believed taking another's life meant destroying oneself. Thus fell the last tribe of the Nation.

The elders look back on the wonderful days of the Nation of Waitaha and cry...

'Once we were numbered as the sands
upon the shore; now we are few.'

This aspect of our past, this wound hidden deep within the people and the land, explains, in part, why Waitaha chose to conceal the story of the Nation for so long. Now with a courage born of prophecy, wisdom and hope they have decided we are strong enough to know the truth and walk it together.

It is time to reclaim the past. Remember the warriors came late to these shores.
The true heritage of this land is peace. Its stone sings of healing and
its spirit cries of aroha - love without bounds.

THE ANCESTORS BEHIND THE ANCESTORS

'Bind the threads of the people
who came down from the heavens... '

In writing 'Song of Waitaha' I believe I have produced the second book first. It takes our history back an additional thousand years, but elders such as Rose Pere tell us of a deeper trail again, of the people who were here before Waitaha. Their story would be the first book. For a while I thought my journeys to North America and Europe and planned trips to South America, Tibet and Africa were opening the way for the first book. The elders spoke of those journeys as trails to the peoples of Waitahanui - the wider world of the peace peoples.

In earlier times there were many parts of the world where people followed the peaceful way. That was when the Mother was the over-arching deity and matriarchal societies were common. There was balance and harmony in them. Later the Mother was put aside, men came to dominate life and thought, and war became an instrument of society.

Waitaha are not ready for the book of the ancestors behind the ancestors to be written at present. So it may not be a thing of my lifetime or even necessary. Everywhere I travel I find people who are piecing the bigger picture together. Perhaps it is already being done by a dozen pens.

Why was this land favoured by the ancestors of so many peoples? Did they journey here to find a safe place to store their wisdom when the peace Nations fell? Where better than these remote islands that were home to pounamu, the stone of peace. While these thoughts fly in the face of the standard histories, they are increasingly supported by researchers who quietly follow independent lines of inquiry into the realms of 'forbidden archaeology'. It's a difficult trail to walk because those with an investment in the standard interpretation wield the power. It is very hard to challenge the accepted story.

Michael Harlow, my thoughtful mentor for 'Song of Waitaha', once said...

> 'Walk the margins, that's where the excitement is, where the truth is found. In the centre is power, control and compromise. Only on the margins do we find the freedom to really understand and grow.'

So I've walked the margins. It's a lonely place but those you meet there are very special people who are opening our eyes to a wider world.

Long voyages without compasses and modern navigational aids have been made in recent decades by the Hukulea the waka of the Hawaiian peoples. They have sailed over 50,000 kilometres on the old sea trails of their forebears. Many waka have now been built in numerous Pacific countries to reclaim the voyaging past of the Polynesians. People like Ben Finney and Nainoa Thompson have made this possible and returned something very precious to all of us.

Thor Heyerdahl, of Kontiki fame, links South America and Easter Island. One day his work will be truly understood and honoured by the world. Fay Campbell, based in Hawaii, has researched old migration routes and mapped, through precise symbols carved in stone, a trail back across North America to Western Europe, the Mediterranean and the Middle East. Kahuna, I sat with in Hawaii, also spoke of an ancestry that originates in the Middle East.

> It seems we have worked hard to limit the voyaging skills of the ancients. In doing so we have diminished them and diminished ourselves.

The TRAIL of the DEER

JOURNEY TO THE RED EARTH

In 1991, in the first draft of ' The Story of the First Woman', I wrote...

'When the deepest of Tides rolled back from the Land, the dark clouds
cleared and the Sun reached out to touch the body of a beautiful woman.
She was moulded from the Red Earth of Kokowai. She was of the Nation
with skin coloured red by the first colours of the rainbow.'

In May of that year Barbara and I were going to visit our son Gordon in Boulder, Colorado, and
our daughter, Anne, her husband, Matthew, and our two grandchildren in New Haven. Yet as
we prepared to go I knew two agendas were being put in place. Two journeys were entwined -
one to the family and one to take the manuscript to the Red Earth to honour the ancestors. Only
when that was done could the book go forward.

From the outset I saw this journey to the desert lands was meant to be. It took shape as quietly
as the walk to open the Peace Trail in 1988. It had the same feeling of everything and everyone
being in the right place at the right time. Money was short but we badly needed the break and
wanted to see our children so the tickets were ordered. A few days before they had to be
uplifted and paid for Barbara received a letter announcing she had won $10,000 in a special
bank account we had kept alive with a few hundred dollars. We had the funds. The doors were
opening.

So it was no surprise to find on arriving in Boulder that Gordon had arranged to take us into the
canyon lands of Mesa Verde, the Needles and the Arches for a week. He had no idea of my need
to take the manuscript into those lands. The Red Earth was calling. An ancient circle was
to be opened again in the desert.

The Kaumatua sent me forth on this journey with a karakia to open the way and an amazing whalebone tokotoko to carry. Few know the age of this magnificently carved talking stick but many have been touched by its power.

Soon after we set out for Mesa Verde I began to feel we were locked into a timetable not of our making. That feeling is difficult to describe. Unexpected things caused delays. We were pulled out of a line of traffic and given a speeding ticket when just over the limit. The details on the citation were confusing and had to be checked out at the traffic patrol headquarters. Everywhere we turned we met little delays. I recognised the emerging pattern. We were being shunted around. This kind of thing was familiar to me now so I tried to relax and waited to see what would unfold. The outcome is often swift and always unexpected.

We crossed a high pass of over 10,000 feet on a four lane interstate highway. It was very busy. Vehicles were speeding by in both directions. Suddenly a deer ran out of the forest, hurtled past car after car and smashed into the front of ours. The poor animal was thrown over the bonnet and into a deep ravine beside the road.

Steam issued from the crumpled front, the radiator was wrecked. The vehicle was not able to be driven but we were unhurt. We were all very shaken. Gordon was deeply upset, devastated to see our journey apparently ended here, anxious about his damaged car and very concerned about the deer. Leaving Barbara with him, I went down the steep slope beside the road to find the injured animal forty feet below.

It was a doe. I hoped she was merely stunned and would soon rise to walk again, but a closer view showed her injuries were massive. Her legs were shattered. Yet she was amazingly calm and turned her head to acknowledge my presence. I sat beside her cradling her head in my lap. I gently stroked it and all the time watched her wide eyes for fear and pain. She accepted my touch and looked at me without distress. I talked quietly.

It's hard to know how long I sat with her. Her closeness, her acceptance and her trust were overwhelming. Yet I knew only one end was possible and that my last act would be one of kindness. I thanked her for the gift of her life. Then wept because my path was one of gentleness. Every part of me cried out in protest. Why was I being asked to kill when that was so abhorrent to me? What did this mean? Deep within I was screaming...

'This trail is too hard. Just too hard! I cannot do what you ask of me!'

Yet I knew with utter certainty this beautiful animal was giving its life for me. She honoured our journey and opened the trail to the Red Earth. I understood nothing of the lore of the trails of this land but saw the wonder of her sacrifice and accepted it. The blade cut deep and set her spirit free. Later I was helped to understand the gift she gave that day. It is always with me.

We came to Mesa Verde two days late in a vehicle battered up front but drivable after running repairs in Durango. The Red Earth was magnificent. Colours woven in bands of time echoed the creation of life. Here the Anasazi, 'the ancient ones', gardened and built their homes. A people of peace who brought life to the land until the warriors came to sweep them aside. They held on in the power of their minds and the strength of their hearts. They refused to take up weapons, to deal in death. And they retreated to the higher ledges of the canyons and used long ladders to reach places of refuge. But the day came when the people and the gardens were no more.

We moved on to the Needles National Park to sleep in the desert, for it was there I wanted to take the manuscript to the Red Earth. Late in the afternoon we left the walking trail and came to a wonderful formation, a rock shelter that was home to families in the past. Stone flakes were scattered over the ground to show where tools had been fashioned. It was easy to feel the spirit of those who once slept within these arching rock walls.

We watched the stars brighten the heavens and went to sleep in our tents. I planned to wake early to greet the rising Sun with the trail prayer and light the trail fire. However, about midnight I was awakened by a sharpness on the back of my neck. I reached around and caught something small and hard between finger and thumb. I remember thinking...

'This may be a small twig, but I think it is alive, so it's important to hold it firmly.'

Half in and half out of the sleeping bag and holding my torch awkwardly in my left hand, I brought the object close and was startled to see tiny crab-like pincers scything through the beam of light. It was a scorpion.

Suddenly the torch, which was activated by pressure on its sides, flipped out of my tiring fingers. As I grabbed for it the scorpion fell from my grasp. I rummaged around but couldn't find it amidst the jumble of sleeping bag and clothes in the shadowed light. Deciding we had already shared the lodgings without real incident I abandoned the search and went back to sleep.

As the darkness began to lift I went to honour the ancestors of the Red Earth with the simple ritual of fire and prayer. Gathering a handful of twiggy wood I went to the chosen ground. I laid the manuscript there and gave life to the flames. As they grew stronger I cupped my hands around them to control the draft. It was but a little fire. Yet as the flames reached higher they sent great clouds of smoke across the rock ledge and over a small canyon.

I was concerned. Someone might see the smoke and alert the Park authorities. This was definitely a non-smoking zone. Yet I could not douse the little fire, the flames had to die in their own time. Gordon came and stood beside me as I looked to the first rays of the new Sun and said the karakia that brought me to this ancient land. It opened the oldest of trails back to the ancestors to bring their children together again as one, that the people of peace might walk again. Everywhere.

Smoke filled my world. Then, on the last word of the karakia, magic moved over the land. Every wisp of smoke instantly vanished. The only remnant of the moment was the small pile of ash within the circle. I gently scattered it across the rock.

It was done. The Old Ones who had gone before us had been honoured. The manuscript had been offered to the Red Earth and the spirit of the land.

There were many unanswered questions sitting all around me. Why had the deer given its life for me? What was its gift? Why was the scorpion sent to me in the night? How would I know the way was open for the writing of the old wisdom to continue?

This seemed to be the end of my journey to the ancestors of the Red Earth, but there was a sting in the tale. Several days later I returned to Boulder with a high fever and terrible pain that raked my body in great waves. This illness was diagnosed in the local medical centre as 'some kind of virus' so I filled myself with painkillers and we flew east to New Haven to keep to our travel schedule.

Still feeling very ill I was trying to enjoy this reunion with the family and to get to know the grandchildren. I was tired from the travel. We had only been in New Haven for half an hour. It was an effort to sit and drink tea. Matthew, our son-in-law, was scanning the weekend edition of the New York Times and interrupted our talk to say...

'Here's a fascinating article about the fastest growing disease in North America. It's called Lymes disease.'

He began reading aloud. Initially I found it hard to concentrate on his words but as he got deeper into the report I was all attention. Eventually my suspicions became certainty and I broke in to say...

'I think I have it. It fits my symptoms perfectly.'

Lymes disease only came to medical attention a decade ago because of the persistence of one woman who refused to accept the explanations given for an affliction that brought great pain to her children. After a long campaign she convinced the medical authorities in Lyme County that something very sinister was abroad in their territory.

The medical researchers who took up the challenge discovered her children and many others had a spirochete in their bloodstream that was a dangerous intruder. It was placed there by the bite of a deer tick.

The article went on to say New Haven was the main centre for research into this disease in the USA. The next day I was with one of the top men in the field. Tests showed my white corpuscle count was critically low. My immune system was losing the battle. I needed immediate treatment. If the 'little beasties' released into my blood stream by the tick got to places where the drugs couldn't follow the situation might be very serious. This surgeon had just implanted pacemakers into two seven year old boys who caught Lymes four weeks earlier. Their 'electrical systems' were malfunctioning and their hearts were failing.

My treatment was successful. It took four or five months to get much energy back and full recovery could be years away. Yet throughout there was a reassuring sense of inevitability about these events. I had returned with the 'Histories' to the Red Earth to honour the ancestors, to seek permission to tell their story. Along the way I had taken the life of a deer, held a scorpion in my hand, said the old prayer to open the trails and seen a great swath of smoke vanish in an instant. I had caught Lymes from the deer, arrived in New Haven the day an article was published on this little known disease, had the piece read to me by Matthew in the city that was the centre of research into it. I was in the hands of the very best in the land. And in the hands of others who moved to tides and time far beyond my understanding.

Despite the problems and the pain I felt I was being looked after. Had I gone home without the Lymes being diagnosed I doubt it would have been recognised soon enough in New Zealand to save me. After all, they had missed it in Boulder where Lymes exists.

When the billowing smoke of the trail fire had vanished the moment the last word of the karakia was uttered, it was as if a voice was saying...

'You walk another path in this land. You are tested each step of the way and you are supported each step of the way.

The next journey was to the Whale People. Visiting the whales was a complete surprise for me. Anne and Matthew organised it as an extra. On reaching the shore I went to greet the waters of the Atlantic Ocean. It was interesting that the tokotoko the Kaumatua asked me to carry was carved from the rib of a whale. It was given in exchange for the beautiful wooden one I'd carried over the Peace Trail in 1988, and thereafter. I brought a whalebone treasure to these distant waters to honour the Whale People, the keepers of the ocean trails. The karakia said to greet the Sun in the Red Earth was now said to the waters.

The seas off Cape Cod should abound with whales in this season but our guides were careful to warn us they could not guarantee sightings. I had few worries about that and was right. So many whales came to visit us that the guides, who saw it all so often, were at a loss to explain their presence in such numbers. But they hadn't seen the whalebone tokotoko. It was a wonderful day.

'Honour the circle.
Honour the keepers of the trails
of the skies, the waters
and the land'

LISTEN TO THE LAND

'The wisdom we need to build the new nation of peace is still there. Some walk it every day. It is the truth within ourselves. It is the music of the land.'

Back in New Zealand I went to Paul, my doctor, and handed over my medical records from New Haven. He suggested we watch the situation closely and leave my body to do the healing. I liked that approach and said I would see Wendy, my other doctor, who was also a homeopath.

When I walked into Wendy's surgery, she shot back in her chair as if in fright. I was mystified by her reaction but said nothing. After briefing her on the Lymes I said I felt as if I was carrying a huge burden and was exhausted. She replied...

'You may think that, but there is an amazing energy all around you. It's filling the room.'

Wendy sat quietly for a time. I said nothing and waited. Then, with an incredible sureness that I find so comforting, she said...

'I have no medicine for you this time.'

I'd had this response on several occasions. Wendy sometimes decided my condition should not be treated with remedies for the body.

'But there are three things for you to do. First, read this.'

She took a book titled 'Rolling Thunder' from her desk drawer as if it had been there awaiting my visit. Across the cover I saw the words, 'An illuminating insight into the mysterious powers of the Indians'... 'Bullseye,' I thought.

'Secondly, hold fast to the old stone.'

My confusion must have been very clear. She immediately began to describe its size and shape. Still mystified I looked in my mind for pounamu to match her detailed description but none I carried fitted. It had to be pounamu, the healing stone. Then it struck me the stone was red not green. It was the oldest of the trail stones - my grandfather stone. The one handed down from century to century to guide the Trail Makers. It was not only healing I needed but direction.

'Thirdly, honour yourself.'

This last task set me back on my heels. What did she mean? How did I set about honouring myself? I left with a book and instructions to greet a stone and to learn to honour myself. This journey ran deep and touched into many realms.

During those months of recovery from the Lymes I had the feeling I was preparing for another role. Although there was in fact two years of writing to complete the book, at another level it was already finished. The one certainty in all the confusion that assailed me was that everything was changing. I was opening up to other worlds around me and beginning to realise this journey began many years ago.

I was sixteen when I first discovered the deep excitement that flows from the land. Four of us had climbed to the top of the Paparoa Ranges behind Blackball, on the West Coast. We were to spend several nights in one of the old gold miners' huts once used by my grandfather. Standing above the bushline with the valleys stretching out far below, I was filled with overwhelming joy. It was as if I had entered another realm, touched something deep within the land and myself. From that moment my life changed. I yearned for the heights, the tussocks, the rocks, the streams and the spirit that moved there. Away from the mountains I felt diminished.

That was the excitement of a spirit at one with its world; knowing its deepest truth, seeing the trails that open the heart and mind to worlds beyond this world.

My historical and archaeological research in the 1970s took me to many remote places in our land. Initially I was rather casual when moving on to old gardens, fortified pa, canoe landing places, villages and so forth. There was work to be done and I got on with it. However, it wasn't long before I was forced to stop and listen to the land. On some sites I felt so at home, so at peace I could stay there forever. Others filled me with foreboding, sadness, pain and anxiety.

To begin with I thought I caused the mood shifts, that the sadness or the joy was of me. However, in time I began to tie my feelings about the different sites to the historical events that took place there; to understand the moods emanated from the land.

Punakaiki, in the Paparoa National Park, Westland, is a very special place, a land of ancient learning and healing. I go there often to embrace the excitement of its rugged shores and feel the overwhelming joy that comes from just being there. It is home.

In Queen Charlotte Sound is Wharehunga Bay. I went there in 1978 to survey the fortifications on the spur with Jim Walker and Murray Thacker, old friends in this line of work. I knew nothing of its history that day. We left the ketch in beautiful weather, climbed the ridge and soon found the defensive walls and house sites. The sheep had grazed it closely so the features were very well defined and our work was straight forward. As we went through our survey an unease began to grow. Half way up the pa, Murray found a native pigeon with a broken wing. We caught it and secured it in a cloth bag and it settled down in the darkness.

With the fortification mapped I scouted above it and found the village I expected to be sited there. This was often the pattern in the Sounds settlements - a village beyond the pa. As we surveyed it Murray became agitated and began to question the validity of the house sites I was measuring. He said we should leave. This was unusual for him. Yet his anxieties were mirrored in me. I also wanted to be off the pa as soon as possible. Clouds rolled shadows across the Sun and darkening skies brought rain as we hurriedly finished the work and retreated to the ketch.

Many months later my research revealed a startling story about that place. Ten of Captain Cook's crew were killed there by the Maori in 1773. Everyone aboard the ship's cutter that pulled ashore died on the beach or within the fortifications of the pa. We will never know for certain what precipitated that terrible event. Maori also died when Cook acted strongly to recover the bodies of his crew. Tragedy shrouds those beautiful hills. The pain of the past still lingers.

So long before I came to the work with 'Song of Waitaha' I was developing a heightened awareness of the land, was opening to its past as well as its present. I sought no answers, no rational explanations for this feeling. It was enough that what I felt was so often confirmed by the research and in time that wasn't even necessary. If I felt a hurt in the land I accepted that. If there was joy there I enjoyed that too.

Yet when I returned with the Lymes disease after the journey to the Red Earth the land took on another dimension for me. This new relationship with the land was different from the excitement that lifts the spirit on the hilltops and different from touching the past.

I discovered some land needed to be healed and some land gave healing. The Lymes left me needing to sleep half of the day. Yet as soon as I got out of the city with its clutter of buildings, vehicles and noise I began to heal. The more I think on this and feel its power the more I wonder why I should be surprised. Are we not born of the land? In the Waitaha creation stories we are born of the clays of the earth touched by the waters and the warmth of the Sun. Papatuanuku, the Earth Mother, is the womb of our making and Taane Nui o Rangi forms and shapes us for he is the life force.

The mother nurtures and heals her young. Even when the cord is cut invisible ties remain. We deny ourselves that nurture when we turn our back on the land and forget the mother in the earth. How hard we have worked to become something that stands above and beyond Nature. Controlling the waters, shaping the land, filling the air with industrial wastes and ripping out minerals.

It is easier to do this if we deny the land has a living spirit. One of the greatest shifts in human development came when the church saw belief in the spirit of the land, the waters, the forests, the mountains and the skies as heresies in the world of the One God. The old ways that acknowledged the spirituality of trees and rocks, that allowed animals to have a spirit, that accepted the stars above as realms of the spirit, that saw spirit properties in water were condemned and those who believed in such 'falseness' were harshly treated.

What sadness that we should so diminish the realms of the Great Spirit, the Unseen One we call God. How strange God should only give the gift of the spirit to people? And how devastating for humanity to be separated from our kin, from the fish, the birds and the trees, and above all else from the Mother and the Father.

In the separation are the seeds of our own demise. Released from the obligation of honouring the spirit of the waters, the rocks, the trees and the land, we are free to use and abuse them to serve our own narrow ends.

Those who followed the old lore respected the spirit of everything. They did not cut down a tree without asking Taane Mahuta for its life. And permission was not always given. Nothing was taken from the waters or the forest without the agreement of the guardians. Furthermore, in the taking there was restoration. When a tall tree was felled for a waka it was replaced by fifteen seedlings and the Tohunga presiding over the felling was responsible for their nurture until they could stand alone in the wind. Nothing was taken to the detriment of the spirit.

So much is being written today of the 'Oneness of Life', the 'Holistic World' that it is easy to set it aside as something trendy, 'something suspect'. Yet in walking away from that kind of totality we narrow our vision and retreat into a smaller place that denies so much.

My spirit lifted when I was able to be open to the power of the land. Later I was to learn much more of this from the peoples of the American Indian Nations. So I began the deeper healing. Late in the winter of 1992, I journeyed through the land in my van, sleeping in the back as the need arose. I returned to the hills, forests and waters of Westland, to the home of my childhood days. I travelled to Nelson and Golden Bay and slept beneath the stars. A lone traveller on a lonely road. I was being healed of the Lymes.

And on the way I met another traveller. The day I left Punakaiki my journey was to sacred waters in Nelson. To honour the old ways, I needed a woman companion to walk with me. Few backpackers were on the move, but a young Irish woman at the camp said her destination was the same as mine. I invited her to travel with me, but said it might be a bit quiet as I was on a journey. She replied she had guessed that already. Nothing more was said.

We travelled through the Buller Gorge in a misty rain that put a cloak of mystery over the land. Later in the day Dympna accompanied me to the sacred stream and understood when I sent the karakia to join with the spirit of the waters. When I set out I'd known a woman would be there. However, if Dympna's appearance was no surprise, her ancestry was. How wonderful that one born to the Celtic lines should stand beside me. Did she journey to meet ancestors who left distant homelands many centuries ago?

The waters brought healing. The mountains and the forests breathed life into me
and the spirit of the deer found a place in my heart.

WALLACE BLACK ELK SPEAKS

'Our prayers rise with the smoke
to join with the four winds
and speak to the skies.'

During my stay in North America I didn't contact anyone within the Indian Nations. No one. The journey was to honour the ancestors of the Red Earth. The prayer to open the ancient trails was sent to them across the silence of that desert dawn.

Eight months later, in January 1992, the words chanted as the smoke rose to greet the Sun were answered. An elder in Christchurch, opened his door one morning to find an Indian standing there. The visitor said...

'Greetings my brother. I am Wallace Black Elk, of the Lakota Nation. I come for the six red stones and the fire stone, that once again we might make the pipe of peace we had 2,000 years ago.'

This greatly respected Indian Shaman, who has done much to share the old wisdom of his people with the world, arrived unannounced at the home of a Kaumatua who walked closely with the book. They had not met before, no letters had been exchanged, no telephone calls and no faxes.

There were so many messages in his words of greeting. I had carried the 'six red stones' into the deserts of the Red Earth. The 'fire stone' he sought was pounamu, the stone of peace and healing. He was saying that sacred stone had travelled from our land to his some two thousand years ago. Old trails hidden for centuries were being revealed again and joined.

Black Elk stayed for two days and many things were shared. I know little of the deeper matters that were visited, but suspect my journey to the Twelve Nations, a year later, had its origins at that time. At some stage Black Elk said...

'I know the sacred knowledge is being written. We support you. I came because I heard the prayer that was said in the desert.'

The words spoken in the red dawn were answered. Black Elk left with enough pounamu to make two peace pipes - one for the Sioux Nation and one for the Waitaha Nation.

The gathering of the old tribes had begun. The way was opening
to the Nations of North America.

CROSSROADS

'This land is washed with tears. It is a sad place; so many
families died here.'

In October 1970 I had a terrible premonition. Gordon my six year old son, was going to be hit by
a car. He was my shadow, where I moved he moved. He knew where everything was. I'd say,
'Gordie, remember that new screwdriver I got a month ago, the blue one, I can't find it.' Off he'd
trot and be back with it in seconds. It wasn't because he hid these things away, it was just that
he kept an inventory of 'things' in his mind. He could 'see' them.

This premonition was so strong that I asked Pete and Anne, who walked him to school to be
very careful. I reminded them daily. During that week I couldn't shake off the 'picture' of the
accident. An anger filled me when I thought of 'the driver'. I said to myself, 'I'll kill the driver if
this child is injured through some stupidity.' It was all very real and almost too much to handle.

That weekend we went to the mountains. The Flemings, family friends, came too, so it was a
very social time. I was able to relax. Then one of the older children rushed in crying, 'Gordie's
been hit by a car.' We ran to the main road. A car was on the verge and people were gathered
around a small bundle in a blanket. Gordie was in a very bad way. His colour was terrible, his
head was swathed in blood. My gut feeling was, 'There's not a lot of time. We must move!'

A voice at my shoulder said, 'We have sent someone to call an ambulance from Christchurch.' It
was the driver. He was standing there in all his pain. Contrary to my expectations, I was
overwhelmed with deep compassion for this man - the one I'd thought I would want to 'kill'. I
quietly replied, 'We can't wait for an ambulance, we have to go to meet it. We need to get him to
hospital fast.' Then, the Fleming car pulled up. While we had all rushed down the hill, Neil had
stayed behind to get blankets and towels. He was ready to go.

We left within moments with Barbara cradling Gordie in the back seat. I was in the front swivelling around, desperately wondering what we could do. After a few kilometres she said, 'Can we change seats?' Somehow we did that without stopping.

I laid Gordie along the seat, crouched on the floor and placed my hand under his clothes and on his bare chest. I could feel his every breath and it was laboured. He seemed to be slipping further away, struggling to signal his body to take in one more breath. I felt the trauma to the brain was so great his senses were 'dulled' to the point where they were barely functioning. He was going too deep.

I decided to try to lift him out of that 'dulling place' by introducing a sharp pain to penetrate the mists around his mind. So I took his hand and used my eye teeth to bite on a finger joint. I did this over and over, finger by finger, sending wake up signals to his brain. And all the time my hand was monitoring his breathing. It was still very laboured and one side of his body was clearly paralysed.

'Gordie, we don't want to lose you,' I said. We were only thirty minutes into the journey, perhaps an hour from help. Then he stopped breathing.

'Neil, Stop! Stop!' Gordie was blue about the lips and his face was drained white. He wasn't breathing. Instinctively, I turned him on his side and as his body came over a clot of food slowly oozed out of his mouth. He began to breathe again. His colour slowly improved.

As we pulled away I glanced up to see where we had stopped and engraved it on my mind. We travelled swiftly on hoping to meet the ambulance soon. By my calculations it should have reached us by now. It never did. When I enquired later I was told they got two calls but couldn't come because, 'They didn't have a name.' I am still baffled by that statement. Things are probably different today.

We reached Christchurch and travelled down Riccarton Road with the horn blaring, hoping to get a traffic officer to escort us. None appeared. Gordie's breathing was still ragged but he made it to the hospital.

It was six days before he regained consciousness in the Intensive Care Unit, and perhaps another ten before he was able to talk coherently. The paralysis down his left side disappeared quickly, but it was a few months before he was back at school again. He needed more than forty stitches to repair the damage to his scalp, but miraculously his skull wasn't fractured.

That was the first time Gordon 'died'. Later an elder was to say 'He is of the twice born, and very special.' I tell this story for reasons I hope will become clearer soon. Meanwhile, I need to share something that happened eighteen years on, in late December 1988. It is another part of the bigger picture I am exploring here.

Sixteen of the family had gathered soon after Christmas for a picnic by a country stream in Canterbury. It was a wonderfully sunny day in a particularly beautiful place. Some were relaxing on the grass, sunbathing, talking, reading, and others were getting ready to swim in the nearby stream. Don and Neil, my older and younger brothers, joined me on the grass. Gordon walked by stripped for a swim, and they both commented on how great he looked. There was a glow about him. It was only a few weeks since we came off the old Peace Trail. He looked so alive.

A short time later Gordon returned, dried himself off, and sat towel in hand on one of the deck chairs. Minutes later Anne cried out, 'Dad, look at Gordie!' Several of us rushed over to him. He was white-faced and beginning to lose consciousness. He was going from us. I knew this was no ordinary sickness. I instantly went behind him and put my hands either side of his head and said very strongly, 'Gordon, Come Back! Gordon, Cooome Baaack!'

He stirred. Became stronger. His colour improved, his eyes cleared, he was shaken but aware. We took him to hospital but found he was in wonderful shape according to all the tests. I was not surprised. This was a sickness from another world.

I thought about our arrival at the picnic. How Gordon had gone to open the gate, which we were assured beforehand was chained but not locked. How he struggled with that chain and gave up, came back and said, 'It's locked.' I said, 'It shouldn't be,' so he went off again and eventually had it open. He returned to the van visibly upset. Gordon hadn't wanted to go through.

When I phoned one of the Kaumatua later that afternoon he left immediately to inspect the stream. Later he said there were human bones in the water. They were of his people. Those who died there centuries ago when the Nation was broken. Erosion along the bank had released them to the waters. He explained...

'This land is washed with tears. It is a sad place; so many families died here.

We must take your young one to the mountains. He has the gift of the waters. There are things to do to help him walk with it.

Meanwhile, I have placed pounamu in the stream and healed the hurt.'

Later, when the Moon was right, we went together to take the uncovered bones of the ancestors high into the hills. Leaving hours before dawn we reached the heights as the Sun tried to penetrate a shroud of mist. The play of the light around the trees and across the hillside was amazingly beautiful. After greeting the ancestors, and taking the gathered bones to join them, we went higher on the ridge to where the Sun warmed our backs. There the Kaumatua blessed Gordon for his work with the waters and gave him the means to protect his gift and himself.

There are strands within these stories that interweave. The place where Gordon was struck by the car, is linked with the place where he collapsed during the picnic. The tie is one of blood. When the Nation of Waitaha fell, the people of peace, who lived for over a thousand years without weapons, died without resisting the warriors. The families gathered their children around them, held hands, formed the circle of peace and awaited the death blow.

That doesn't mean they died without pain and deep anguish. The terror of those last moments is unimaginable. The hurt wrought there remains in the land, in the bones that were left to whiten in the Sun, in the memory of those who grieved for the end of the Nation.

Families of the Nation died in that mountain location and beside that stream on the plains. Gordon nearly walked to his death in both places. The blow he received from the car was the blow of the club of the warrior. The death that touched him in the waters was of the bones of those who died. I puzzle over this but find comfort in knowing that when Gordon stopped breathing after the car accident he was given life again within one of the great healing centres of the Nation of Waitaha.

When I was on the stone trail to the Indian Nations in 1992 I raised some of my anxieties. I asked this of the wise ones...

> 'I fear for the life of my son. I have given him life twice and I'm afraid I may not be there if he needs me again.'

> 'You have given him the gift of life three times,' was the response. 'That is all that is allowed of you. Others will care for him now. Do not be fearful.'

Yes, I had given him life three times. I was his father. However, something tells me he was giving his life for me on both occasions.

I know 'Song of Waitaha' was 18 years in the future in 1970 when Gordon was hit by the car. But I also have this sense of time folding over time. How was my son's life woven into mine and into the trails of the ancestors?

I know my years of childhood were touched by events that seemed to mark me for the work with the sacred knowledge. During the writing of 'Song of Waitaha', when I was voicing the 'Why me?' question yet again, an elder said...

> 'Someone dedicated you to the work when you were very young. We don't know who, but it was done.'

Later, in pursuit of an independent answer, I asked the same question on the stone trails, and the wisdomkeepers of the Indian Nations came back with the same answer. Only this time there was more...

> 'The one who did this did not understand the mind of a child. A burden was left that was not intended.'

Kaylynn Two Trees, Wallace Black Elk's granddaughter, added another dimension to all this for me. She explained that an Indian male child who is born to walk to the sacred crossroads, to take on difficult work for the people, is taken from his mother at an early age. She tears her garments, scars her body and mourns the loss of her little one for four days. The child is now bound to no one, he is of the people.

This struck a deep cord in me. I had been taken from my mother at birth because of her illness and spent many months of my early years with relations and friends. I am sure I was wonderfully cared for and loved by those who sheltered and fed me. But I was not bonded to my parents in the usual way.

There was much to think about. When I spoke to other elders of the deep loneliness I felt, they said...

'That was how it had to be. It was necessary for your journey.'

Coincidence, accident, destiny, fate? Was my whole life a preparation for the work? And what of my children? Is the journey written at birth? Are there real choices on this river of life?

At the age of eleven I stepped barefoot into the stream near my home and the waters ran red. I was horrified to discover I'd lost most of the flesh beneath my big toe. The doctor asked, 'Where is it, I can sew it back.' Of course it was gone, but its significance surfaced much later. My injury ran back to a very ancient stream.

These were tapu or sacred waters. It was the stream to which those dedicated to be the Pae Arahi, the Trail Makers, were brought at the age of ten or eleven. Here a foot was marked and the blood allowed to flow into the waters of the taniwha. Forever after, that footprint would be like no other in the land. It was unique. Thus were they initiated into the lore of the trails, and challenged to lead those called to carry the pounamu across the mountains.

I had stepped into that stream at the right age, and I was later called to lead the twelve who journeyed to open the ancient Peace Trail that the stone might move again.

My son Gordon was born in Nelson. As a babe he splashed around in a sparkling stream beside our home on the road to Lake Rotoiti. He loved that place and little knew the power it brought into his life. Think on this. Gordon's degree is in Physics and he began his work as a 'water scientist' with the Institute of Nuclear Sciences. He tested the purity of water, analysed trace elements within it, calculated its radioactivity, was able to show that some rain that fell in the Southern Alps 100 years ago was just reaching the streams of the Canterbury Plains today.

The Water People of Waitaha, sought one stream against which to test the waters of all others in this land. This was the stream they chose. The waters Gordon immersed himself in as a babe were those sacred waters. By chance Gordon became a 'water scientist' and tracked the water trails beneath the surface of the land and came to measure the purity of the waters of the world.

Gordon's two encounters with death happened at a crossroads in time, at places where the sacred winds of the past broke through into the present. A few months ago, in January of 1995, I returned to the Peace Trail to guide another twelve over the mountains and walked into another mystery. It adds life to the questions raised here.

There is a place on this trail where we pause to greet the most ancient of rata trees. Thereafter it climbs steeply and steadily to the distant Styx Saddle. I have made that climb three times but one of these was very different. The first was in 1961 with old friends, Rod and Marie, and the second in 1990 on a wonderful Commemorative Walk for the youth of this land. On that occasion, sometime after we left the old rata trees, I became intrigued about the trail. I have the kind of trail memory that records pictures of the journey in great detail and can usually reconstruct them years later. This time the pictures I held from 1961 didn't match the trail we were walking in 1990.

I was feeling really strong as we climbed with the young people chosen to carry greenstone over the old trail. Very strong and mystified. Then, without warning my energy fell away in seconds, and I slumped to the ground drained to the depths of my being. Jo and Derek came back to sit with me. After a while I recovered and moved on. We reached the saddle in good time.

But the question I ask now is, 'In whose time?' You see, when we walked the trail again in 1995, and came to the ancient rata trees and greeted them and moved on, the trail we followed was that of 1961. It matched the mind pictures I carried from that journey. The first journey and the third followed the same ground but the middle one was different.

Where did we walk in 1990? Did we walk part of the old trail of centuries ago, a piece of the past gifted to honour the young walkers who came to celebrate the achievements of the ancestors? Had time and space moved to honour our footsteps? Were my attempts to reconcile my memory map of 1961 and the pictures of this trail in 1990 too much for me to handle? Did I straddle time too precariously and fall between to experience instant exhaustion?

If we returned to that section of the trail of today, and beat about the scrub, I don't think the trail we walked in 1990 would be found. It existed long ago. It still does, but not as we might expect to find it. My mind tells me this cannot be so, but my heart and spirit say otherwise.

I paint a large canvas here. The Wise Ones tell me I know the answers to the questions I place before them. That is so, but leprechauns have short memories when they dance the trails of the rainbow.

The TRAIL of the EAGLE

THE CALL TO THE HOPI

'Those who are called to walk to the sacred crossroads are favoured by the gods. Yet it is a hard journey that takes them far from family and friends to test the borders of their courage in the loneliest of places.'

Two people far removed from all these events, and quite unknown to Waitaha, were responsible for the next joining of the trails. Wendy Brown of New Zealand became stranded in Sedona, Arizona, when her money and passport were stolen. A stranger in a strange land. Friendless and alone and sleeping rough, she was aided by people who led her to the Hopi where she was given shelter.

This chance beginning led her to discover her 'Hopi Family'. From that moment she dedicated herself to bringing other New Zealanders to meet the Hopi in what became 'Wendy Brown Adventures'.

Meanwhile back home Wendy told Dr. Cornelius Van Dorp of her links with Hopiland. He had been working as the medical officer on various Greenpeace voyages in the Pacific and in Antarctica. He was constantly drawn to the peoples of the Pacific Rim and was writing a book of his adventures.

During a visit to the South Island they met with Sam Karaitiana of the Waitaha people and were intrigued to hear his story. The Waitaha connection seemed to run back through the Pacific to many peoples visited by Cornelius. They asked if he would send a message from Waitaha to the Hopi when they made their next visit to them. Sam agreed.

Wendy was very surprised when she received a stone in the mail. It was a piece of pounamu shaped by the waters of the river. So this was Sam's 'letter'. When she gave it to the Hopi it was accepted with great joy and laughter by chief Martin Gashweseoma...

'My, these people have a great sense of humour,' he said Then very softly added: 'You will bring the man back in May.'

Sam was the obvious person to go but it wasn't possible for him. Meanwhile Cornelius had been in touch with me. He was very excited about what he had learned of 'Song of Waitaha' and wanted me to go to the Hopi with him. For several months he kept in touch, but I was desperately trying to meet a publisher's deadline for delivery of the 'Song of Waitaha' manuscript and couldn't see my way clear to go.

However, within days of Cornelius's departure for the Hopi an agreement was reached with the publisher to hold the book over. That freed me to go but my financial situation was very tight. However, Ellie came into the picture to make it all possible. Earlier we had gone together to the Clyde Dam site when they closed the sluice gates and Lake Dunstan was born. We arrived to find hundreds of fir trees, willows and poplars drowning in the rising waters. I felt the pain of it all. No one had told the trees what was happening.

We did what we could to heal the hurt. I said the karakia and a great wind swept through to shake the autumn leaves from the willows. They swirled about and floated down like a golden rain. When I looked to the Sun it was encircled by an amazing rainbow.

It was Ellie who went to Air New Zealand to see if they could help us get to the Hopi. They had already given strong support to the book. When they said they would provide a return ticket I was able to go. I only had one day at home in Christchurch to prepare for this journey. I felt at that time the trail ran to the Hopi, then down to Peru, Chile and Easter Island. Air New Zealand talked with Lan Chile Airlines and obtained agreement for tickets on that leg as well.

Over the previous months I'd discussed the possibility of going to the Hopi with the elders and they had said very little. I was not to know until much later that the stone which went to Wendy had not originated with Sam at all. It came from the Kaumatua who had been with Wallace Black Elk.

With the way now opening I asked the Kaumatua if this journey was to be made. He said...

'It is all in place, the wairua moves. You are to go.'

He arrived soon after with the tokotoko to be carried on this journey. It was an old friend, the carved wooden one I carried to open the Peace Trail across the Southern Alps in 1988. The whalebone tokotoko that had gone with me to the Red Earth was to stay behind.

Then my mind turned to the pounamu I would take to the Hopi. I didn't think there was any left in the storehouse but Barbara returned with twenty pieces from which to choose. Some were quite large. As I sat trying to decide which stone would travel the Kaumatua intervened and gathered them all into a pile and said...

'Take it all. Go to those who carry the greatest pain and have the deepest need.'

When the Kaumatua left, something that worried me surfaced. On my way home from Auckland to pack, I'd seen my son Gordon in Wellington. I'd told him of my plans over the phone earlier. He'd answered the door, and I felt a weight in him. He held me tight and wept saying...

'If you go to South America you will not return.'

He was very upset. I assured him my plans were not set, and I would listen to his words. In the rush of preparation I'd forgotten to raise this with the Kaumatua. It would be hard to find him now so I decided to phone a friend who might be able to help.

I told her of the journey with pounamu for the Hopi, then said...

'I also think I'm going to Peru and Chile.'

'The most dreadful feeling has come over me', she whispered, 'Don't go to South America! You will die there.'

I respected their intuition and would look deeply into the needs of the trail before stepping into those tormented lands. While that door was not closed, it certainly had a large warning sign on it.

So I set out with twenty stones for Hopiland, but the first one found a home long before we reached there. My first thought was to go straight to Hopiland with Cornelius but I decided to go to Kauai first to relax with Wendy Brown Adventures. That was a good decision for two reasons; I was to meet a wonderful group of people who were all healers in their own right, and I came unwittingly to the oldest of the islands of Hawaii.

One of the stones was destined to stay in Kauai. I didn't know that when I arrived there. Yet it became very clear when our guide on the dolphin voyage off the Na Pali coast pointed out an ancient sacred place nestling beneath tall mountains rising out of the sea. It called out strongly for the stone.

However, the greatest surprise of all came when it was time to choose the stone to leave on Kauai. Maruhaeremuri Stirling of Te Whanau a Apanui, was with the party. She had come to study the herbal remedies of the Kahuna and the Hopi. As women are the keepers of the pounamu I asked her to select the stone to be gifted to Kauai. I spread them all out on the floor and she immediately chose the stone to stay. She picked up a second stone and said...

'This is to go to the Fire Clan of the Hopi.'

That was very helpful. She held a third stone and it was only then that I began to realise what was happening. She said...

'Lake Titicaca...mokihi rafts... fish, people, feathers... the old ones... the Sun God... sacrifices.'

Messages were coming to her through the stones. The next said...

'Piwaruwaru... Pocohantus... woman... water clan... brimestone... Nevada.'

We stopped. I was taken aback by the information, yet it sat well with the teachings of those who carried the old knowledge. Greenstone has often been referred to as 'our old recorders'. Was it some kind of receiver that captured thoughts sent across time and space. Like the crystal in the old 'crystal radio' I had as a boy?

On a beautiful morning the stone for Kauai, and the partly finished manuscript of 'Song of Waitaha', were taken to the sacred place on the Na Pali coast that had attracted me from the ocean. It was received amongst the ruins of that old school of learning by Auntie Angeline, a gentle and joyful Hawaiian healer. Three women stood beside her to honour the path of that stone. That afternoon she was to carry it to the Kahuna elders. We were given two stones in return and healing salt. Another of the ancestral trails was touched by the stone again. A gateway was opened.

It was a few days later in Los Angeles that Maru returned to hold the remaining stones. While she sat with them and spoke the messages, I wrote them down. It was clear three stones were for the Hopi - one for each of the Hopi Mesas. Then they began to run through the Indian nations of the deserts, plains and forests. The Paiute, Shoshone, Crow and Cree, Lakota, Chippewa, Huron, Cherokee and Choctaw were clearly represented when she was finished.

I had left home thinking my journey was to the Hopi and then to Peru, Chile and Easter Island. Now the stones were laying down a completely different itinerary. I didn't have any clear idea where the Indian Nations named were to be found. Soon after we flew on to Sedona. There the design became clearer.

The Sedona experience was remarkable. It's hard to describe the things that happened without seeming a 'bit strange'. However, my approach to the sacred knowledge was very open. I knew deep down if I challenged knowledge or occurrences that were outside my experience, if I closed down when confronted with phenomena that defied the rational, I would learn very little.

This openness didn't happen overnight. There was a long period of 'deprogramming' before I was in a suitable state to be taught anything that really mattered. However, by the time I reached Sedona I was more comfortable about listening to my heart and going with it. Sometimes my mind still got in the way but I was seeing this earlier and adjusting.

Sedona is awesomely beautiful. We went in the early morning to an amazing place of worship built on a ridge and backed by immense, canyon cliffs. I sat facing the cliffs for a long time fascinated by the shapes and colours within the stone strata. The head and body of a giant tuatara suddenly emerged from the rock face. It was born of the interplay of shadow and stone. I loved that image for the tuatara is the keeper of the sacred knowledge. Then two eagles appeared to drift across the sky and disappear into the distance. What wonderful friends to meet as I began the journey with the stone.

We moved on to a very sacred place called Bell Rock. It was a tall butte of great power. Sixteen of us gathered on the great rock platform at its base and formed a circle. I said the prayer to open the trails, the same one said to the Red Earth the previous year. It would sound again and again in the sacred places of this land. The wairua flowed strongly. When the karakia ended most left to climb the steep slopes of the hill.

Eight of us stayed behind. We sat around. All was still and quiet. Something tugged at my mind - there was another prayer to be said and a ceremony to be performed. Five of us formed a circle. One was Robert Archer of the Cherokee Nation who was to be so important for us in Sedona. The others were Greta and Philip who were going on to Peru after the Hopi, and Cornelius who was our leader in Sedona.

I said a karakia for the stone and put my greenstone pendant into the earth, lifted it to the heart and then held it high to the heavens. Three others had pounamu with them. I blessed it for the trails ahead and spoke of their journeys. Then at the end we joined hands and these words came to me unbidden....

'Fly like the soaring eagle. I set you free, I set you free, I set you free.'

We then drifted our separate ways. Jenny and David, who were sitting outside the circle with young Sam, came and asked me if I realised that when I said the karakia it was held within the circle. No sound escaped to reach them. I was not surprised. It had happened before.

However, it was Robert Archer's question several days later that threw me. He asked...

'Do you know a young Indian man fell to his death on Bell Rock four days before we stood in the circle?'

'No!' I replied in some confusion. I wondered, Why Robert was asking me this?

'Ken told me about the tragedy today,' he explained, 'And it brings some answers to a mystery that has been with me since we left Bell Rock. And it raises other questions.'

Robert explained how he described the ritual in the circle of five to Ken, a friend who was close to the old lore. He did this because something teased a thread of memory that he couldn't quite grasp.

'When Ken told me of the accident I began to understand. Do you know you performed the critical part of the Indian Spirit Ladder ceremony when the five of us were in that circle? It was done on the fourth day, the right time to set the young man's spirit free to return to the stars'

I knew nothing of the death and nothing of the Spirit Ladder ritual. It was a matter of innocence or perhaps 'inner sense'.

Robert took me from Bell Rock to his home to attend to a pulled muscle in my calf. It had been with me for some days and was a nuisance. I lay on a massage table as he worked the soreness out of the muscle. He said 'Who would want to throw a spear into your leg?' I replied there were people who did not want the 'Histories' to be published. He responded with, 'Laugh at the robber barons. Don't take them seriously.'

Then I told him about the Lymes Disease. He tested me and said I was not yet fully recovered from its effects. My immune system was still not in top order. Then he took an Indian drum and said to relax and journey with it. He beat out strange and beautiful rhythms that took me back through history to many peoples. There was one theme. Over and over I saw the slaughter of the innocents, terrible acts of genocide. Although it was difficult, I remained outside the terror until I came to 'Wounded Knee'. For some reason that hurt cut deep and I wept briefly. Then I travelled the world through time to the end of nations. And I found the deepest shadows in Africa where I came to a darkness I could not penetrate.

Some would say I had travelled with the drum through past lives. I do not know of these things. But I do know I have grieved for the death of nations for as long as I can remember.

As I came out of the drumming I sat on the side of the table while traditional herbs were burned for the smoke to drift about me. All sensation then went to the soles of my feet and they began to pulse in a powerful way. This was the strangest of feelings.

As I relaxed after the massage Robert shared a moment that he found very strange...

'When you wept for those at Wounded Knee it rained heavily out of a clear blue sky.'

Several other wonderful healers came to help me during the next week. I felt I was being prepared for a long journey but I still didn't have the itinerary details. At this stage I was somewhat bemused by the words given by the stones. What did the cryptic clues mean? Where were the Indian Nations mentioned located? Was the stone really going to them? Would I take them? My life was a fantasy novel, a kind of cosmic joke.

The beginning of the answer came a few days later. Friends, and friends of friends we had made in Sedona gathered for a quiet party. As it came to a close, Alan Leon, a wilderness guide, offered to take any who were interested to see the Sun rise on an ancient vision wall.

Five of us met him before dawn. We walked into a valley and at first light Alan stopped to chant a brief Indian prayer. I said a karakia. As we moved on I saw Alan glance at me with questioning eyes. A little later he stopped, rummaged in his daypack and came over with a beautiful crystal. He asked, 'Will you carry this for a while?' It fitted snugly into my hand. I thought little of this as we hurried on to be in the right place to see the wall when the Sun hit its face.

I saw no vision in the hour we spent before the wall, but it was a wonderful place to be in the early morn. There was something special about this crystal I now carried. It was comfortable to be around, a strong friend. When I gave it back to Alan at the end of that lovely morning he said nothing. However, six weeks later he was to confide that I was the first person to hold that stone in 14 years. He had dipped deep into his medicine bag to bring out that sacred treasure.

Alan was of Choctaw blood. He had spent years in the wilderness of Montana and came into town one day to hear one of the old Indian shaman speak. He found it difficult to find parking and arrived late. The old man was in full flight so it was an awkward moment because the only seat available was right in front of the speaker's lectern. He made his way across to it and, as he sat the old one stopped and said...

'How good it is to see you. I have been waiting for you to arrive.'

None of that made any sense to Alan. He was a stranger to this man. At the end of the talk the shaman approached him and said...

'I am getting old. I need you to climb some mountains for me. They are very high mountains but you can do it, even if you have to carry stone.'

Alan was stunned, but he met the old one again as arranged and agreed to climb some mountains. And he did. He carried stones to heights few see and journeyed into realms only the shaman know. He was taught the old knowledge of the stone and more besides. That is a little of his journey and I leave it there in the hope we may share Alan's story one day.

Alan of the Choctaw, our guide to the vision wall at dawn, arrived that evening with the words...

'I hear you have a problem with some stones. Would you like me to try to help?'

That afternoon I'd purchased an old map of North America. It was very large and drawn by hand, perhaps a replica of something produced in earlier years to excite the imagination of the young. Across it were drawn many trails with hand written notes beside them. One said, 'end of the Shoshone trail'. That was what had taken my eye. They were the very words Maru received from the stone. Nations named by her were also there, 'the Huron, Cherokee and the Crow' to note a few. In places it marked the sites of old battles.

We went to it. We were like children with a treasure map - Wendy, Cornelius, Maru, Alan and I. In fact the map was of very little help. It set the stage but the drama was in Maru's words and Alan's understanding. As I read the words Alan pondered. He found a location and I placed a stone there. It all happened quite quickly. There was no hesitation or discussion, the stones went down one after the other. One was placed in Canada, one in Montana, another in Utah, and so on. It was a mesmerising time. I was stunned to see a great circle of stone appear on that map.

It was the sacred circle, the 'circle of the dream'. It was to be created in pounamu, the healing stone. I remembered the Kaumatua's last words when I'd left...

'You go to plant a seed. The stones go to those who carry the greatest pain and have the deepest need.'

Shivers ran through me. There was a powerful wairua in all this. Then it really hit home. I had to make that huge journey. How could it be done? Even more important, how was it meant to be done?

It became clearer. There was old wisdom to guide us. We needed a 'hand' to carry the stone - that meant five people. I immediately asked Alan if he would be our guide. He said he would need to go into the hills to find the answer. Cornelius, Wendy and Maru were all keen to go. A great adventure was unfolding. The problem now was finance. None of us had the funds to make such a long journey.

I could think of only one person who could help find the money needed. I phoned Judi in New Zealand. She had supported the book in the past when we got into a really tight corner. She understood the pain of peoples who have suffered at the hands of others and saw the world with the eye and heart of a poet.

I worked out a budget. We needed $NZ 7,000 to travel that great circle of 8,000 miles in a van, and allow for accommodation and food. Judi's response to my hurried words on the phone was...

'There's no corporation in New Zealand that will fund that kind of thing. I'll see what I can do. Can you phone me again tomorrow night?'

I don't remember this being an anxious time. Everything was too big to worry about so I just had to get on with it. That night Judi said she would provide the money herself but it was all tied up for some months. Would that help? It was a wonderful response. Barbara arranged the funds through her lawyer from her mother's estate and put them into my visa account. We were able to go. It was now a matter of who and when.

Alan returned from the hills after three days away and said, 'I am to be your guide.' He asked if we could be ready to leave in ten days time. He had much to do.

Many people came with gifts for the journey with the stone. Robert Archer's healing help and his instruction in Indian lore was to be very important. Robert Shapiro, an author, well known in Sedona and much further afield, was another who became a wonderful guide and friend. A gentle man of ideas, he brought an old wisdom to the journey that lay ahead and arrived one day with another gift. It was a beautifully tanned elk hide to wrap around the pounamu. Ken came with tobacco to present to the elders of the Nations. Jenny arrived with a swatch of sage to burn, and a length of naturally carded wool dyed an amazing red to be used as my headband.

James Yax and Janneke Verster gave me two white swan feathers; prized treasures from the Netherlands, their homeland.

There was more healing. Catharine Suerth, an expert with Indian drums, used that power to send me into a deep healing sleep. Then La Mere came to hear the story of the stone and dance for us. Within minutes she danced Maru and me into another realm. All I can say is that I could see an old Indian village with all its sounds and smells and smoke from the fires. Maru's experience was the same. We described the same place. In many remarkable ways we were being helped to attune to the long trail ahead. Meanwhile we had to go to the Hopi.

'Learn to reach beyond yourself and be shaped anew, the real world is the world of the spirit'

GRANDFATHER TITUS

'This is my power. I am honest. I do not steal. I feed the Sun. I plant the corn that
gives us life. I honour the Great Spirit. I do not say one thing and do another. I am
of the one hearted people.'

Robert Archer played a larger and larger role in this venture day by day. So, when he suggested
I go straight to Hopiland with him, instead of going to the Grand Canyon with the group, I
agreed. Robert was of Cherokee blood and a gifted healer who was well versed in the shamanic
way. Our trip to the Hopi took all day because Robert wanted to share his culture and the sacred
places as we travelled.

We went to the valley where the 'earth breathed'. I stood over a hole in the ground in the desert
on a perfectly still day and heard the air rushing in and out of the depths of the earth. The
outward breath was so powerful it would seize a handkerchief held in the hand and stretch it
skywards like a streamer. We went to the ruins of villages with wonderful stone walls. They had
been deserted for centuries but the pride and presence of the old ones remained.

Eventually Robert brought me to Grandfather Titus. He went straight to the old one and began
to ease the pain in his joints and was very pleased with the improvement since his last visit.
Titus said he was now able to return to his fields.

I sat quietly on the floor outside the conversation but knew Titus was well aware of my
presence; he seemed to see nothing yet see everything.

The treatment over, we sat cross-legged opposite each other on the floor. Titus was very small
and wiry. Some say his age is 112 years. He is old, yet timeless and chief of the Hopi. One of the
few great ones left.

Silence. The old one looks through me to some distant place. Not a word. No eye contact. Still no acknowledgement of my presence.

When I felt it was right I placed the stone on the floor. It was born of the mountain waters of the Poutini Coast of New Zealand. Grandfather Titus asks to hold it. With caring hands he caresses it, following the rounded surfaces smoothed by rock grinding rock in the flood-tides. Touching it to his cheek and forehead he closes his eyes for a long time and opens them to say...

'It is of the light of the Sun, the stars and the Moon.'

He returns the stone. Others will receive it for his people. Then he reaches out to hold the finely carved tokotoko, the one the Kaumatua brought to me on the eve of my departure.

Again the gentle touch, the intent examination, the long silence as he holds it close. Again it is returned but this time he looks steadily at me searching, seeking, knowing. I say...

'Grandfather, now I will tell you my story,' and began to speak of Waitaha.

'Stop!' he said very firmly, and raised his hand, palm towards me. 'I know your story. I know of your people, I know everything about you and your journey. I have listened to the talking stick.'

Then to my amazement he proceeded to show his understanding. Yes, he knew all about me.

It was a very special moment. The tokotoko had spoken as in the old times. I had written of this in the 'Song of Waitaha', but thought there were few left who could hear it speak. The ways of the Medicine Men of the Hopi and our Tohunga were one.

I have written this account as if Grandfather Titus was fluent in English. That was not the way of it. While he understood what was said he found it hard to form the words quickly in response. In fact for a short time his daughter translated for us from Hopi to English.

However, she left and Grandfather Titus led us across the room to sit once again cross-legged in a tight circle. For awhile nothing was said then he startled me by saying in his very slow, deliberate way...

'If the government throws me in prison, or men come against me with guns, I will not be afraid. Their power is nothing.'

His tone was quiet but defiant. He was challenging the world that had dealt so harshly with this people of peace.

'This is my power. I am honest. I do not steal. I feed the Sun. I plant the corn that gives us life. I honour the Great Spirit. I do not say one thing and do another. I am of the one hearted people.'

Now he laid out his sacred stones, feathers, beads and a small hooked stick and his medicine pipe.

'This is my power', he said as he handed each to me to hold.

It was a great honour. These treasures were his very life, things sacred beyond price. He continued...

'We are few. It is the time of great change. Time to heal the land and heal the people.'

Taking the red stones of the Trail Maker, that I carried for Waitaha, and my four hawk feathers I put them in his hands. He held them close and began to pray. In the power and rhythm of the chant the old man became young again. His voice grew strong and sure to fill the room. His chant went on and on weaving into my being, joining realms beyond my understanding.

When he finished I reached across, held his hands in mine and said the old karakia for the trail. The wairua moved through me like a deep tide. There was remarkable strength in the wrinkled hands of Grandfather Titus.

We spanned time to join two Nations as one. As it was in the beginning so it was once more, for Waitaha are of Hopi and Hopi are of Waitaha. There are those among the tribes whose beginnings were of the Red Earth, the desert lands of the ancient ones, who are brothers and sisters of the Hopi. They once shared the same dream bound within the stone. It returned again to lands it travelled so long ago.

Then Grandfather Titus used his hands to make a circle. He did this several times. I couldn't follow the idea he wanted to share...

'Is that the earth?'

'Yes.'

'What is your concern Grandfather?'

He created the circle again and turned it rapidly. I began to think he was saying it would speed up, but my question frustrated him. I hadn't understood. He persisted, saying...

'The shadows sent by the Sun no longer fall as they did for my father. On the shortest of days the shadows stop in a different place. On the longest of days it is as if the old stones have been moved.'

Ancient marker stones on the mesa charted the seasons. The 'shadow trails' within them were changing. Something was clearly wrong. Titus began to use his hands to spin the circle again. I still didn't understand that message.

He saw this and called out and a boy of ten or eleven appeared. After quiet words the lad ran off. We waited. He appeared after sometime carrying a globe of the world. It's hard to imagine where it came from, but there it was. The old one seized it with delight, held it before me and simply turned it upside down.

Grandfather Titus had been telling me the earth could turn upside down. That a polar shift was beginning. And when I questioned him further he explained that only the one hearted people can save the earth. By this he meant those who walked in truth. The two hearted people said one thing and did another. He went on to ask, 'Are there enough one hearted people to make the difference?' In that moment he seemed close to despair.

We sat for hours. The night gathered and it was time to go. Titus turned to me and said...

'Leave more than a footprint. You may be the one who leads others into love and understanding and living at one with the Nation. Use your gifts well.'

Grandfather Titus wept quietly as we left. It was very hard to go. I promised to return. The circle began here and closed here.

We left for Sedona that night. It was only a two hour trip but we took much longer. Robert was about to share one of the greatest of treasures - enroute we were going to the sacred spring in the Washington Mountains. I really didn't begin to take in what he intended until we left the ute at the end of the dirt road and began to walk through the forest in the dark. We had no torches and I realised that was by design. He moved swiftly uphill, sure of the twisting trail. In time I gained the confidence to move as he did. Slowly my eyes adjusted. Then the Moon appeared to light the way. We climbed for a long time in complete silence.

We stopped a number of times for Robert to check the way. He explained...

> 'The last part is the most difficult. We have to find a fissure in the side of the mountain. It's hidden. Few know the way to this spring. Everyone thinks it's on the other side of the mountain. That's not true. The old ones are great at quietly giving out misleading information. Wait here.'

Robert disappeared for a long time. I sat and enjoyed the Moon that was so bright in this mountain air. He returned and said, 'I've found the way.' We came to the fissure. In the distance I could hear water but it didn't issue from this opening into the heart of the mountain. Again he said, 'Wait here.' This time he disappeared into the darkness before him. Another long wait, then a distant chant echoed from the opening. Silence. He reappeared...

> 'The way is open for you now. Go straight ahead and feel your way.'

I stepped into the darkness before me and began to feeling my way into the mountain. It became a very easy journey - even beautiful. I moved slowly, crouched low, feeling the stone that surrounded me, using it to guide me, accepting the darkness and excited about what lay ahead. I understood why Robert made the journey alone and granted me that experience. At last the rock rose above me to allow easier movement, and I came to a band of stone at the height of my shins. The sound of rushing water was just before me. I reached out and touched into its coolness - the sacred spring was at my feet.

It was wonderful to chant the karakia within the heart of the mountain, to offer those ancient and sacred words to the stone and the waters. I thought of the journey ahead, about being here, embraced by walls of stone. I filled a bottle of water to take to the pounamu each day as we travelled to the Twelve Nations.

We almost ran down the mountain. So much was happening so fast. We were soaring on the trail of the eagle. An exciting world awaited us.

'All wisdom is of the circle.'

MARTIN GASHWESEOMA

'Our people have always known of this green stone of your land. It is a great
and sacred stone, a stone of the gods, the stone of peace and love.'

He came into the room and sat down. He didn't acknowledge me, just talked quietly with
Manuel who had offered us this room to sleep in. It was attached to his workshop where he
crafted fine silver pieces in the Hopi way. It was like meeting Grandfather Titus all over again.
Being seen but not seen. That same feeling that I'd become invisible. There was no disrespect in
this; if anything I felt our meeting was being honoured by this distancing.

This man was Martin Gashweseoma, the keeper of the sacred tablet of the Hopi Nation. His life
was dedicated to honour one stone. It was in fact half a stone. The matching half that fitted the
break across the centre had been taken westward some 2,000 years ago by the great White
Brother. Tradition says he voyaged far on the great ocean but one day would return as the
Pahana. And he would proclaim his arrival by the matching tablet he carried. His return would
signal the return of the ancient wisdom and mark a turning point in the history of the people.

We sat across the table from one another. No introductions. Martin folded his arms high across
his chest in the favoured Indian way. Although he spoke good English, Martin proceeded to
speak in Hopi and Manuel translated. Thus began one of the most intense and exhilarating
three hours of my life. Our minds locked together, bonded, talked without talking. I didn't
move a muscle. Martin sat as if carved in stone.

There was little need for words. His question, 'What is this time?' My response, 'It is the time
when there are to be no more secrets.' Silence. We travelled back and forth, over and around,
through and beyond those words. Silence. Everything that matters here is not being spoken
aloud. The questions merely open doors. 'Who are your people ?' I do not respond for many

minutes. That is expected. After all he received the Waitaha stone a year ago and heard its message. He was the one who said, 'The man will come in May.' Well, the man had come.

'Why do you come? My answer was in the words the kaumatua gave me the night of my departure. I replied, 'Merely to sow a seed.' Silence. We entered deep rivers of the mind and found waters to nurture that seed. There was trust here.

'What do you seek and what do you bring?' He was enjoying this contact on the other planes. 'I seek nothing. I bring the greetings of the Waitaha elders, the healing stone, the sacred knowledge and myself.'

I decided to ask something of him, 'Who am I?' Manuel translated this into Hopi and Martin quietly took it in. This time there was no delay, 'We know who you are but it is for your elders to tell you. We cannot do that.' So that door was shut.

The unspoken exchanges went on and on and only stopped when one of my friends interposed with a question. Manuel was very upset by this. He said...

'You have no idea of what is happening here. You have broken it. It is finished.'

Martin left soon after and we were next to meet at their sacred Prophecy Rock at dawn for the gifting of the pounamu. That was quite a different occasion and after the ritual of the stone was over we all went for breakfast. Martin wore a smile, he had shifted into another gear.

We then took greenstone to the three Mesa. Three sisters, Mary Alice, Triva and Bessy accepted one at Kykotsmovi. Tears of joy flowed. The stone fulfilled a prophecy made by their father years ago. Their dream was to rebuild Oraibi, the oldest inhabited village in North America. Their father knew of the islands of the Maori and the healing power of the 'green stone'. 'One day it will come to you', he said. It had come, and at a time of great need. The older ones, like themselves,were finding it hard to work the cornfields a thousand feet below the Mesa. Just walking there and back each day was becoming a huge effort. The younger ones were turning away from the traditions and losing their path in the confusion of the modern world. They were not interested in cultivating the corn which was life itself.

The last stone for the Hopi went to Auntie Carmelita. We sat with her in the Sun and listened as she shared her dream for the future of her children. Later, as we were about to leave, her nephew asked me if we might pray for him to beat his drinking problem. He was twenty, had a wife and child and was imprisoned in a bottle. Maru held him close as we prayed. When it was done a great clap of thunder boomed through the heat of the day. The startled young man looked as if he had been given a very clear message.

Even the Hopi, who say they are the keepers of the soul of the world, are under fearful pressures today. They number only 10,000 and are confined to three small mesa. Surrounded by 400,000 Navajo they try to hold on to the old values and continue to follow the ways of peace that have been their heritage from the beginning. Yet their children face enormous stress and are torn between two worlds. How long can they hold on to their story?

'If we lose our story, we lose our dream and if we lose our dream the spirit dies.'

JOURNEY TO THE TWELVE NATIONS

'Seek out the tribes... they will be expecting you... you will be recognised... teach them of the trail of the heart.'

Alan, of the Choctaw Nation had gone into the wilderness for three days to see if he was to guide us on this journey with the stone. His return with a smile that said, 'Yes' was very important for all of us. Grandfather Titus had opened the way. Alan would be there to guide us.

Our first stone was to go to the Valley of Fire in Nevada. This was the land of the Paiute. Alan led us into the rich red canyons of that valley and on foot to a wall of stone carved with ancient symbols. Beneath a beautiful picture of five people holding hands he set out his medicine bag. Carefully unwrapping the deer hide outer he revealed a huge bear's foot with long sharp claws. It had a section of the tanned bear skin still attached and this was wrapped around his sacred treasures. Amongst them was a large eagle feather. He used it to fan the small fire he had kindled to burn sage for cleansing. The smoke was sweet and sharp.

We sat cross-legged on the fine red sands. Alan invited us to share in the purification of his medicine. Slowly, with deliberation and respect, Alan brought each of his crystals and stones to the sage smoke. When all were done he prayed and then turned to us and said...

'The journey began with last night's eclipse of the Moon and ends with a partial eclipse of the Sun.'

That could mean two months or two years as far as I knew. It seemed a comforting indeterminate time but of course it wasn't. Alan continued...

'That gives us fifteen days from last night.'

I was shaken. How do we travel 8,000 miles (12,000 kms) by van in fifteen days and along the way find the twelve people who are to receive the stone?

Our itinerary was based on the clues Maru read in each stone. I had them recorded in my diary. At first they seemed incredibly vague. We came to the Valley of Fire because the stone said, 'Piwaruwaru.... Pocahantus.... woman.... water clan.... brimstone.... Nevada.' We knew we were in the right state but had gone with intuition to let 'brimstone' bring us to the Valley of Fire. Tracking down the stonekeeper of the Paiute still lay ahead of us.

And when we had completed that puzzle there was the next which offered...'The Shoshone Trail... cauldron... black iron pot... red deer... tall fir trees... snow goose honking...' This then was the challenge. To put in place that huge circle of stone in fifteen days. We needed guidance. Then I remembered the words of Bear Claw, one of the old ones, who said...

> 'Dance the stone trail for you will only succeed if you go with fun and laughter. Scuttle quietly along like little mice. Move quickly here and there, do not seek attention, or you will be stopped.
>
> It is a dangerous trail. Some may seek to halt you.'

Later I thought back to that warning when we were locked in a holding building on the US border, surrounded by five armed guards and waiting to be searched. Yes, some may seek to stop us.

Yet I knew others waited to open the way and receive us. Bear Claw had instructed me to...

> 'Seek out the tribes and let it be known why you are there. People see into the heart. They are expecting you. You will be recognised. Feel at home wherever you are.

You walk with the spirit of the deer. She gave her life for you and the gift of gentleness. And more.'

Day 2. On the stone trail. We found Flora Simmons at home caring for her grandchildren. She was caring for baby Kimberley, and little Gordie, Monica, Christine and Amber. It was hard for her to cope with their questions for they were deeply upset and confused by the recent death of their father. Her son had died a week ago, aged thirty-one. She grieved for him, wondered about the future of the young ones and faced the world with courage.

A beautiful young woman at the Indian Reservation Office at Moapa had sent us straight to Auntie Flora when she saw the words given by the stone. She had no hesitation. It was all very clear to her. We were not so convinced until grandmother assured us she was indeed the one to look after the stone.

We went outside to do the ritual of the gifting and looked over a dry land to distant horizons. When the ceremony was finished and the stone was in her hand she held on to me for a long, long time. The others gathered around when they saw she was on some distant journey and joined her in that closeness. She was utterly still for many minutes travelling in a timeless place, perhaps seeking strength for the days ahead. I recalled the words of the Kaumatua on the eve of my departure from New Zealand...

'The stone goes to those who walk with the greatest pain and have the deepest need.'

In Moapa that hot afternoon I was overwhelmed by the depth of this journey and the wonder of the healing of the stone. As we departed Auntie Flora gifted one of her stones, gathered from the distant hills, in return for the pounamu. It was done. The Hopi stones were joined to the Paiute. The children wanted us to stay but the road beckoned. We had to find the snowgoose honking at 16,000 feet in the lands of the Shoshone Nation in Wyoming.

That night we drove until dark and slept under the stars in a riverbed near the town of Hurricane. Apparently you can't do this in the States because we awoke to be asked by the owner of the waterway for payment for the privilege.

Day 3. The Shoshone Tribal Office in Fort Washakie, Wind River, Wyoming, was where we began our next search. John Washakie, their council chief welcomed us and heard our story. He was very comfortable with the messages within the stones and took us into the conference room to wait while he went to get someone who would help us.

A tall, dignified, white-haired man returned with him. He was Starr Weed, a tribal elder. In fact the one who sat within the council to guide the people on the trails of the spirit. We told him our story in more detail and gave him all the clues...

> 'The Shoshone Trail... cauldron... black iron pot... red deer... tall fir trees... snow goose honking... 16,000 feet... red sunset and red dawning... chief riding horse... seen over and over again... strange halting gait... feather bonnet down to the shoulders only... feather tips black or dark brown... red in the middle... raccoon... swift flowing stream... porcupine.'

He quietly took us through each one and quickly showed us we were in the right place. The 'cauldron or iron pot' was the great dark pit outside the town resulting from iron workings. The snowgeese were flying over the mountains, the swift stream was nearby, and so on until he came to the feathered headdress and the horse moving with a strange gait. Here he smiled saying...

> 'There is only one such bonnet amongst our people. It has feathers with the colours you describe and only comes down to the shoulders.

The horse appears each year. It walks that slow halting way because it is in a parade and surrounded by many hundreds of people.

It is my horse and my feather bonnet. I am the stonekeeper you seek.'

In the grassed courtyard we gave the stone to earth, water and sky. Then the trail prayer was sent into the clear blue above and the stone was placed in Starr Weed's hands to be carried for his people. Before we left he taught us some of the sign language of the Nations. There was much to learn here but the trail awaited us.

Before we left I visited the grave of Sacajawea, the incredible Shoshone woman who guided the Lewis and Clark expedition of 1804-1805 across the Rockies to the Pacific Ocean. She carried her new born babe with her and endured great hardship. It was her trail lore and courage that saw the party survive the mountains and the winter snows. It was an honour to be able to greet a truly great Trail Maker. Another circle was joined.

The dream called us to Montana. We drove towards the night, seeking the Crow. When the stone we left with the Shoshone spoke of 'red sunset or red dawning' it described exactly the skies that gathered as the Sun went to its home in the west. The completeness of this day was written large upon the map. The range we climbed was named 'The Porcupine'. The last piece of the puzzle was set in place.

The mountain lands of Wyoming and Montana were filled with great power and presence. Their beauty was mesmerising and drew my mind back to the alpine wilderness of home. We were far from the waters of the pounamu, far from family and friends yet never alone on the journey. Every day was filled with miracles. The trail opened before us.

Cornelius was at the wheel of our waka. His dedication to a life of adventure and the enjoyment he found in seeking the answers to the message of each stone was wonderful to share. He and Alan were skilled navigators along the trails of many realms. They shared the driving to cover huge distances each day to meet the call of the stone. Yet everything was done easily. Speed limits were carefully followed as they flowed over the land guiding our waka effortlessly through the tides.

Maru was born to lead and born to hear the voice of the stone. On this trail she was joined by ancestors who spanned the ages to open the way. The blunt, humorous honesty she laid upon us on occasions was sent with equal directness to the Old Ones who woke her in the night. Her delightful irreverence brought joy to the journey and helped us all dance the trail. She kept us close to the earth. When we were far from those early days in Arizona she confided with a wry smile...

> 'In the beginning I wondered why the elders didn't send a Kaumatua to carry the stone. You don't have the language or follow the usual protocols. You are something else again and I don't know what that is.'

I agreed with her. I wasn't a Kaumatua just a messenger. A delivery boy sent to travel an ancient trail as best I could with gifted companions to make the journey possible. I was just something else again. Perhaps that was my strength.

Wendy supported Maru. They brought the balance of women to the work and held the waka on course. The Peace Trail was walked in the mana of women, they were guardians of the stone. Wendy had given up a glamorous life in the corporate world to walk the sacred places of the earth. She lived in trust with little money but time to know the excitement of the world.

Alan brought wide horizons to this trail. He saw the universe from the mountain tops and had walked the shaded valleys. He described the wilderness as his home, and travelling beside the rivers and through the forests beneath the mountains, as a prayer. He guided others into the canyons to share the land and his vision. That was his work. Meanwhile each evening he unrolled his blanket and slept on the floor or the ground. Rarely did I manage to rise before him in the dawntime. He waited in darkness to greet the first light of the Sun.

Day 4.. Joseph Pickett, vice chairman of the Crow Tribal Council welcomed us warmly to the Crow Agency. The people were about to perform the four day Sun Dance ceremony and there was great excitement everywhere. The story of the stone added to this. We were overwhelmed with offers of help. Latona Old Elk, a remarkable young woman, who had already spent time in Washington as the ambassador of her people, invited us to stay at her home that night. Her interest in our journey was high for she was of the stone people and had gone with Tom Yellow Tail to carry a sacred stone to the Hopi.

The Sun Dance was a very special ritual that called for months of training and preparation. So we felt greatly honoured when we were invited to take part in it. We felt so at home. These people had opened their hearts to us completely. They were very special and I was soon to learn why.

The command to carry the stone to those who 'walked in the greatest pain and knew the greatest need' had brought us unerringly to this place. The Agency was on the Little Bighorn, the site of Custer's last battle. The place where the Indian Nations made their stand to defend the sacred Black Hills. They were called Paha Sapa, the centre of the world, the lands where warriors could speak with the Great Spirit and follow their vision quest. The government made a treaty with the Indians that stated...

> 'No white person or persons shall be permitted to settle upon or occupy any portion of the territory, or without the permission of the Indians pass through the same.'

> _____ Treaty of 1868

Several years later, when prospectors discovered gold in the Black Hills, the army sent a thousand pony soldiers under General Custer to make a reconnaissance. This was done without any attempt to obtain the consent of the Indians. Sitting Bull responded to this invasion by armed troopers, with these words....

> 'We want no whites here. The Black Hills belong to me. If the whites try to take them I will fight.'

Hundreds of prospectors followed the trail that Custer's supply wagons cut into the sacred hills. Gold opened the floodgates to a white tide that swept ever deeper into the heart of the Sioux lands. The Indians responded with these words...

> 'When the prairie is on fire you see the animals surrounded by fire; you see them run and try to hide themselves so that they will not burn. That is the way we are here.'

This tragic situation culminated in the Battle of the Little Bighorn in 1876. The land was stained with the blood of many Nations. Here the pain of wars that tore the culture of the people to shreds lingers on to visit those who remained. It was there at every turn as we drove the high road of the battle. White stone markers walked across the gentle slopes to show exactly where each trooper fell. Named to commemorate each loss, they spelled out the sad legacy of the red tides of war.

The Crow acknowledged that heritage of pain and dedicated their lives to the ways of peace. None commented on the fact that nothing had been placed in the land to mark the fall of their braves. Forgiveness, compassion, understanding and a determination to build a better community for all peoples was their dream.

The power of this came home to me when we went at sunset to see the Sun Dancers enter the huge lodge specially built each year for the ceremony. Fully robed in the manner of the Crow, splendid in every way, they stepped into the circle to fast and sing for three days to honour the Sun.

My eye was drawn to a woman in her seventies. Her hair was white and beautifully braided. Her clothes were trimmed with wonderfully worked colours and her rug was a joy to see. I asked Latona Old Elk who she was...

> 'She is a Roman Catholic nun. This is the seventh year she has come to honour the Sun. There are others who support us in this way.'

My heart sang. So many wonderful people are reaching out to bring understanding and healing to the world. Nearly half of those who entered the Sun Dance lodge were white people.

The stone called to go to its keeper. We knew early on who that was to be, for the words given were...

> 'Crow people... black feathers... white feathers... beaded with orange, red and brown... bound together... graceful on top...'

John Pretty on Top, a tall chief with beautifully braided hair, was the one. He was within the lodge leading the Sun Dancers to answer the haunting beat of the drums. We could not enter. So the stone was placed in the hands of Jerome Whitehip until the days of singing to the Sun were over.

Day 5. In the darkness before the dawn we gathered outside the lodge to support those within. One side of the great circle opened to the east. The first rays of the returning Sun would travel that path into the lodge. The drums gathered a new urgency as the light grew stronger to reach a peak of power as fire lit the distant horizon. Then the beat slipped away into a quieter place to allow song to greet the light. The people once again honoured the return of the Life Giver and gave thanks to the Great Spirit.

Our leave taking came soon after dawn. We followed a stone that spoke of...

'sadness... red bandana and Wounded Knee...'

It urged us to answer the call to the sacred lands of Wallace Black Elk's people in Dakota. I suspect he is the architect of this circle we travelled. If not the sole designer, then at least a leading partner in a dream created with the Kaumatua who sent me on this journey.

The village of Pine Ridge, Dakota, is our destination this day. It breaks the symmetry of the circle but with reason. Early in my journey into the trails of Waitaha the Kaumatua said...

'What you think of as a mistake is merely a kink in the circle of life. Accept it, let the pain go, and as the circle turns, it will of itself return to its fullness.'

The circle is the dream. Honour the dream and the circle turns to heal the hurt. The lore brings everything back to its essence, to its true shape.

Early in the 1970s I read 'Bury My Heart At Wounded Knee' at our cottage in the mountains. It changed me, opened doors and perhaps in some strange way brought me here. It told the story of a small band of Sioux who were led by Big Foot. The plight of his people is described in this way...

'There was no hope on earth, and God seemed to have forgotten us. Some said they saw the Son of God; others said they did not see Him...

The people did not know, they did not care. They snatched at the hope. They screamed like crazy men to Him for mercy. They caught at the promise they heard He had made.

The white men were frightened and called for soldiers. We had begged for life, and the white men thought we wanted theirs. We heard that soldiers were coming. We did not fear. We hoped that we could tell them our troubles and get help. A white man said the soldiers meant to kill us. We did not believe it but some were frightened and ran away to the Badlands.'

_____ Red Cloud

On December 17, 1890 the War Department issued orders for the imprisonment of Big Foot because he was on the list of 'fomenters of disturbances'. He was ill with pneumonia but was struggling on to get his band to Pine Ridge and Red Cloud's people. On December 28, his party was surrounded by four troops of cavalry under Major Whitside, who herded them to Wounded Knee. The Major's official count on arrival showed there were 120 men and 230 women and children. He treated them with consideration and saw that Big Foot, who was spitting blood from his damaged lungs, was provided with a warm tent. Two troops of cavalry were placed as sentinels around the Sioux teepees and two fast firing Hotchkiss guns were sited to rake the length of the Indian camp.

In the darkness the Seventh Regiment arrived under Colonel James Forsyth and set up two more Hotchkiss guns. This was Custer's former regiment. Some wondered if revenge was in their hearts. Around the fire the officers gathered to share a keg of whisky to celebrate the capture of Big Foot.

At dawn the cavalry mounted, surrounded the camp and brought all the men to the centre of the circle and asked them to give up all their weapons. This was done. Then the Colonel accused them of holding guns back and made a search that revealed two more. This was followed by a body search and a scuffle that led to a shot being fired. The defenceless Sioux fled and the Hotchkiss guns opened up.

'My grandfather and grandmother were killed as we crossed the ravine, and then I was shot on the right hip clean through and on my right wrist... after the soldier picked me up... a little girl came to me and crawled into the blanket.'

These were the words of Hakiktawin, a young woman who survived that day.

When the guns were silenced 153 Sioux lay dead. Many others had crawled away to die later. It is thought 300 of the 350 men, women and children perished at Wounded Knee.

The wounded Sioux were placed on wagons and taken to the church at Pine Ridge. They numbered 4 men and 47 women and children. They entered to find the Christmas decorations still hung over the Chancery and a crudely lettered banner said... 'PEACE ON EARTH, GOOD WILL TO MEN'

One young Indian who walked the horror of that killing ground later wrote...

'I did not know how much was ended. When I look back now from this high hill of my old age, I can still see the butchered women and children lying heaped and scattered all along the crooked gulch as plain as I saw them with eyes still young. And I can see that something else died there in the bloody mud and was buried in the blizzard. A people's dream died there. It was a beautiful dream.....the nations hoop is broken and scattered. There is no centre any longer, and the sacred tree is dead.

___ Black Elk

The past still sits raw upon this land. The people speak of those terrible moments at Wounded Knee as if they occurred yesterday.

At the Pine Ridge Agency we received a warm welcome and were greeted by the words, 'It is time for the broken hoop to be mended.' We were immediately taken to a gathering of grandmothers who met each week to advise young mothers and fathers. They were part of the Foster Grandparents Programme.

I was informed somewhere in their midst was the one who would carry the stone. When I told the old ones the story of our journey they all looked to one elderly woman. It was agreed that Emma Kills Enemy was the keeper of the stone. Emma received the pounamu into her 85 year old hands with a smile. She knew the needs of her people and met them by driving 100 miles each week to give her wisdom to the young ones who sought guidance.

They proudly told me two hundred teenagers were at this time high in the sacred hills on their vision quests. Their young men and women were standing tall. The wounds were healing.

Cornelius was waiting at the van. He had been on his own little trail and found a young man named Tim Thunderhorse who wanted us to go to Wounded Knee. He said one of the elders would meet us there and it was so. Zack Bearshield waited for us in that place where so many died in 1890. We exchanged gifts on the slopes above the valley. The Sun shone brightly and gave lustre to the greenstone I gave into his hands. I thought back to when I first read the sad story of this place. Another circle gently closed.

Day 6 and 7. Our path lay north to the Cree. Two stones were to go to this Nation. The clues were very open. One stone said...

> 'Cree Nation and water... mountains... ducks and snakes... once tied to the Hopi... Grand Canyon... tobacco... peace pipe... wagon trail.' The other... 'Butte Canyon... Cree Nation.'

We had little to help us narrow the location we sought. Although the ancestors of the Cree may once have lived in the lands of the Grand Canyon, Canada was now their home. We couldn't find anyone who had heard of Butte Canyon and it wasn't on the maps. Maru listened to the stone again and said we had to cross the border into Canada.

The only Cree settlement we could locate was hundreds of miles north into Manitoba. Nothing was coming together but we headed for Swan River, travelling in hope and pleading to be told if that was not the trail. Two hours into that journey we drove into a tremendous rain storm. We slowed to cope with sheets of water on the road. Then we got the message.

Lightning forked through the darkening skies and struck the ground just metres from the van. We were blinded by brilliant light and deafened by incredible thunder. Shaken we stopped to think this over. Then I realised the tokotoko for the trail, the carved talking stick that was my constant companion, was not in its usual place. We could not go forward without it.

I felt sorry for the drivers. Two precious hours gained and two lost and we would be back where we started at the border. No one complained. It was all part of the journey. We were being asked, in a rather forthright way, to consider other options. The tokotoko was found in the care of a cafe owner who said he knew it was very special. I can't understand why I took it inside, because it usually only appeared for the ritual of gifting the stone.

These stones spoke of 'canyons' and they didn't fit this part of Canada. Maru said the direction to take was north-east. There we would find the stonekeeper. That course took us to the city of Winnipeg. When we entered Winnipeg the tall buildings created the 'canyons' mentioned by the stone. That seemed a step in the right direction, but finding the Cree in this sprawling metropolis was going to be a huge challenge. We spent a day using telephones to contact different agencies such as the Native Clan Organisation and the Aboriginal Council of Winnipeg and hour by hour narrowed down the search as one name occurred several times. David Blacksmith was the young man we were advised to meet. David was thirty-five and a field officer with an agency for youth. We sat in a circle on easy chairs. Youths came in and out and ten or twelve eventually gathered to listen. David welcomed us. I briefly told our story as it had now been told many times. This was greeted by silence. I placed the pounamu before me and left it in full view. I didn't know this was to be the most difficult discussion on this long trail. It lasted nearly two hours and opened wounds that ran very deep.

'Why do you bring the stone?'

'It is a gift for your people.'

'What do you want from us?'

'We ask nothing of you.'

The floodgates opened. David spoke with moving intensity. He said...

'We have been given other gifts and suffered for them. Alcohol has stolen our will. Drugs have eaten up our minds. Everyday we rescue those whose lives are destroyed by these terrible gifts. Others we bury when they decide to leave. Education has taken the best and brightest away from our culture and given them life without soul.

You say you ask nothing of us. That has been said before by academics who came to help us, but in the end used the wisdom shared to win themselves university chairs. Our culture has been defiled by some, stolen by others and distorted to confuse our children.

Come with us this evening to the old ones and they will test the truth in you. Are you brave enough to let the snake learn the ways of your heart? You bring stones. I do not wish to accept the stones. Take them with you.'

We listened. The pain he felt for his people was very strong. I quietly acknowledged it and remembered the words of one of the old chiefs of the last century...

'They made us many promises, more than I can remember, but they never kept but one; they promised to take our land and they took it.'

Now I told my own story to David and his people. I spoke of opening the old trails within Aotearoa, of my journey into the old wisdom and the sacrifices. I shared my hurt and opened my heart. In the end the words didn't matter. He looked for something else. I had not tried to persuade him to accept the stones, I merely shared a little of my life, tried to find the place for our paths to meet.

David sat in silence once more. Looked at me, at the others who had not spoken at all during this discussion, and came to a decision. He left us. It seemed the stones would go elsewhere. Then he returned with an eagle feather and placed it before me. This was a great honour. As I accepted this symbol of the soaring mind and spirit from the Cree, David lifted up the two stones. We walked the trail of the one hearted people.

Day 8. Winnipeg fell away behind us as we headed for Thunder Bay, the Great Lakes and the Ojibwa Nation. We travelled through a wonderful world of forested lakes and small islands. It was a magical landscape. Later in the day our route straddled the Canadian - United States border and forced us to enter the United States twice before breaking free for the journey to Sault Sainte Marie in Canada.

The hours ahead of us I still recall with utter amazement. At the US border post we were asked to leave the van immediately and step into the interview room. I was in my socks but wasn't allowed to return for my shoes. Our passports were taken by someone who began to access a computer. Meanwhile everything was being unloaded by uniformed officers who carried sidearms. We were asked to identify our packs and sit there while they were searched. Every item seemed to be regarded with suspicion.

When my pack was cleared I glanced out the window to see the officers going over the empty van inch by inch. The Cree eagle feather dangled from the sun visor on a cotton thread. To carry such a feather drew a mandatory $5,000 fine. The trail was rapidly descending into swamp lands that threatened to stop us here and now. I remembered the words of the old one...

'Dance the stone trail... Scuttle quietly along like little mice... do not seek attention, or you will be stopped. It is a dangerous trail. Some may seek to halt you.'

We had not sought attention but we were certainly getting it. Alan was next to have his pack searched. It was very small for he travelled light. The officer opened the top wide to reveal the huge bear paw that folded over Alan's sacred, bear skin bundle. He didn't see those huge bear claws. He saw nothing as he reached around them three times to dig deep into the pack to feel through the clothes. This was powerful medicine.

I waited to be questioned about the eagle feather. However, that wasn't the next step on this journey. One of the officers who was working on the van entered carrying the ash tray. It seemed to be empty but when another officer tested a small corner of ash with a chemical kit it changed to the colour of danger. Someone had smoked marijuana and left a trace behind. We carried no drugs. The van was a rental. The 'evidence' against us was another's folly. This suggestion carried no weight. Cornelius, who was the registered hirer, was formally charged with the offence and informed this carried a $1,000 mandatory fine. He was asked to pay a $100 surety to allow the van to be released back into our care. The court proceedings would follow later.

I waited for the feather to fall upon me. Nothing was said of it. Had it blown away when all the doors and windows were opened during the search? No! It was still there proudly waving in the breeze. Visible to some and invisible to others.

As we left one of the officers quietly told Cornelius it would be very hard to pursue this matter when he was back in New Zealand.

A little later we re-entered Canada with great relief. What we had just been through was both frightening and reassuring. As our lives were walked through by the officials I felt a terrible powerlessness. We were ordinary people going about our business, respected in our own land for our work, but on this occasion caught within a net intended for others. The atmosphere of assumed guilt that surrounded the whole procedure was hard to shake off. Yet we had been protected. The trail opened before us.

Day 9. We approached the US frontier once again. This time we saw no one except the officer who sat behind a large window. A loud metallic voice asked us to drive along the arrowed line and stop outside door five. We approached it and stopped. A great steel roller door went up and we were beckoned inside. The door closed behind us. The steel door in front of us was shut. Six men carrying guns stood there to greet us...

'Please get out of the vehicle and stand alongside the bench. Touch nothing. Do this, now!'

There was no time to think. There I was standing in my socks again and this time it was on cold concrete. The officer across the table was watching me empty out my pockets. I felt like a naughty boy caught in the act, but my pockets revealed nothing to catch his interest. Now comes the body search, I thought.

The officers sweeping through the van were all over it but the feather had flown to another place. It was hidden far from view, safe.

'Return to the vehicle', was the next instruction. My frozen feet responded quickly to the invitation, even though the path might lead to the place where they would search my person. The steel door rolled up. The officer in charge said, 'That's the way', and pointed to another arrowed road. It was only when he wished us a safe and happy journey I realised we were free to go. I had scrambled into my shoes for nothing.

Thunder Bay, on the shores of Lake Superior, opened the way to Sault Sainte Marie and the Garden River First Nation Reserve, home of the Ojibwa who are also known as the Chippewa. We followed the flight of a beautiful bird for the stone spoke of a...

> 'Dark blue shining bird... glinting colours... another shade of blue showing through... raised feather on its head... heron or huron... blue waters... stream... waterfall... canoes and people... village on the flats... feather standing up... brown tip... off-white in the middle... Running Bear... Moon Flower Maiden.'

This little stone had much to say. That was often the way of the little ones. It called us to Lake Huron where we hoped to find its keeper.

Day 10. Willard Pine welcomed us to the Garden River Reserve and said the one to meet was Marlene Pine. She joined us at the tribal council table and heard our story. Then she said...

> 'I've been waiting for you to arrive. I have known of the coming of the stone, it was seen in the smoke of the fire. This morning I knew this was to be a very special day.'

Then she turned to Maru and said...

> 'I am also a woman of the stone. Walking with it is often very lonely. It is wonderful to meet you, my sister.'

We had found 'Moon Flower Maiden'. All the other wonderful clues were not needed. They had been swept away by the swirling smoke.

Marlene said we must find Grandfather Daniel Pine. Consternation crossed her face. She explained her problem...

'Grandfather is 92 and confined to a wheelchair, but the people have purchased him a van and his son Patrick is his driver. Now days we never know where he is. He just disappears and reappears with a smile and no explanations. I'll ask the office if they have any idea of his movements but I don't hold out much hope.'

She left and we sat there drinking coffee hoping against hope we could meet the old one. Marlene returned smiling...

'You will not believe this. For the first time in memory grandfather has left a detailed itinerary for his morning movements and contact phone numbers. He told the office they just might need to get hold of him in a hurry. We can be with him in a few minutes. He is heading for home now.'

Grandfather Daniel Pine had just returned from the university where he had shared the old wisdom with the students. He was in his sunset years. One arm had been removed at the shoulder and he was unable to walk. However, he was still very strong in spirit. I could see why the people loved him. He was still walking his vision. He lived to hand his knowledge of healing to four young ones before he died. This vision was recorded on tape. We felt very privileged when he played it and shared his deepest aspirations. The Ojibwa had responded to his dream by building a Medicine Lodge to his specifications to provide the sacred space for the teaching. It was soon to be opened.

We sat around the table talking. He listened to our story but made no move to open the way for the stone to go to Marlene. He asked me...

'What time is this?'

'It is the time when there are to be no more secrets. It is time to share the old wisdom. It is the time of the prophecies.'

'Much is going to happen. It will be good,' he said.

He asked Marlene to get some 'medicine' from the fridge. She produced a large jar and five glasses. Grandfather was about to share his medicine with all of us. He poured it. Five small portions and a sixth that was very large. Mine was the odd one out. It was made from herbs and tasted very bitter. One sip would have been enough to satisfy my curiosity but that wasn't what he had in mind. Under his watchful eye I downed it all. What need did he see that called for this attention? Did the legacy of the Lymes disease reveal itself to those old eyes?

Grandfather signalled to Patrick, his keeper, and was carried outside to a fire that smouldered in the middle of a circle of log stump seats. Marlene's earlier words returned... 'It was seen in the smoke of the fire... I knew this was to be a very special day.' The old Medicine Man made the sacred smoke and sent a prayer to travel with it to the skies. He invited me to gift the stone to Marlene. He then asked her to listen to the stone and share its message, but when she held it close nothing came. I sent her a silent thought... 'Take it to water.' She responded aloud saying, 'I'll take it to water.'

Now the stone spoke to her with great colour and power. She talked without stopping for about fifteen minutes and all the time grandfather sat nodding and smiling. I knew where Marlene journeyed. This was a glorious pageant of the ancestors with vivid descriptions of costume and colour and place. She filled the land with images of peoples long gone from us. Then the old one felt her tiring and suggested she stop.

Meanwhile the word had gone out and the family was gathering. Food was being carried in by many people. Willard appeared, and the sisters and brothers gathered, to begin a spontaneous celebration of song that lasted well into the afternoon.

The leave taking was difficult. Grandfather Daniel Pine wept at the parting and asked me to return for the opening of his Medicine Lodge.

Somewhere in the south another Nation waited to receive the stone. It knew the way. The message was clear and very poetic...

> 'Come down from the Chippewa
> On the acrid trail
> where the eagle flies
> You will hear the cry
> as Tecumseh dies.'

Tecumseh was Shawnee and this was his message to the Indian Nations...

> 'Where today are the Pequot? Where are the Narragansett, the Mohican, the Pokanoket, and many other once powerful tribes of our people? They have vanished before the avarice and the oppression of the White Man, as the snow before the summer Sun.
>
> Will we let ourselves be destroyed in our turn without a struggle, give up our homes, our country bequeathed to us by the Great Spirit, the graves of our dead and everything that is dear and sacred to us? I know you will cry with me, 'Never! Never!'

Day 11. We travelled late into the night to reach the Huron - Potawatami Nation near Lake Michigan. They were few in number but their very existence now came from the courage of others. In the last century when the army arrived in force to drive Huron and Potawatami west, the white settlers of the town of Athens took the Indians into their homes and hid them until it was safe to return to their villages. This tide of gentleness that stood against the guns left a legacy there that is honoured to this day. Tecumseh's cry was heard far beyond the lodges of the people. Not all were moved by avarice.

An old women of the tribe spoke to us of these things. The memory of those days was kept alive in her stories. She said we should take the stone to the tribal centre at the Pine Creek Indian Reservation. It would find its own trail from there. We performed the ritual of the gifting of the stone with John Chivis, one of the young leaders of the new Nation. He promised to place it in the hands of one of the old ones who knew the ways of stone.

Day 12. We were racing against the Moon to finish this trail, travelling long hours into the night, often getting only five or six hours sleep. This was necessary if we were to have daylight time for finding the stonekeepers and sharing the journey. The Cherokee of the Smoky Mountains now sang to the waters of the stone. The one we carried wept for that Nation. We were about to visit again the 'trail of tears.'

These eastern tribes were the first to feel the weight of white settlement. By the early 1800s many tribes were gone forever and others were in serious decline. The great Cherokee Nation had survived wars, whisky, disease and increasing settler pressure for a hundred years, and still numbered several thousand. All that changed when gold was discovered in the Appalachians. In 1838 General Winfield Scott's troopers rounded them up and created holding camps. A few hundred escaped to the Smoky Mountains but all the rest were herded west to the Indian Territory as winter descended. This became the 'trail of tears of the Cherokee' a terrible journey of over a thousand miles that saw one in four die of hunger, cold or disease.

We entered the Appalachian Mountains and climbed steadily through forest blurred by shifting mists and came to the beautiful Smoky Mountains in bright sunshine. Jonathan Taylor, chief of the Eastern Band of the Cherokee was at the hospital where his six year old grandson was seriously ill, having suffered a brain seizure. The message we received from him was that he would meet us at 6.30 am for breakfast if the boy was out of danger.

We carried two stones for the Cherokee. One for the Nation at Smoky Mountain and the other to travel to the Western Band in Oklahoma. Every two years the 'trail of tears' was crossed to bring the people together.

Day 13. Jonathan arrived with the news that the child was doing well. We shared the breakfast hour and soon after he accepted the stones at the Reservation Centre. He spoke proudly of the dream of his people. They were determined to hold together and looked to the tools of the modern world to achieve this. Using their own television station they beamed into every Cherokee home the meetings of their councils and anything else that needed to be shared.

This early start freed us for a long day on the road to reach the Choctaw of Mississippi. That day we spent 17 hours on the road. Midway through that journey we came the Choctaw Reservation Centre at 5.00 pm. We came there in the forlorn hope we just might find someone to help us. The complex was deserted. No one. Completing the circle before the partial eclipse of the Sun was now looking very difficult.

As Alan switched on the motor to pull away and find a motel for the night a car pulled up and a young woman ran inside the Centre. I followed her and waited at reception. It was some time before she reappeared and my presence was a surprise. She introduced herself as Thallis Lewis. She was anxious to be gone, but waited politely as I spoke briefly of our mission. Then she sat down and said...

> 'All this amazes me. I never return to the Centre in the weekends. Yet here I am and our paths cross. I'm here because one of the elders has just died and the list of those to inform immediately was filed here.

I believe I am the one you seek. I am the Cultural Director of the Choctaw. My learning is with an old one of 95 years. She walks with the old medicine and has chosen me to follow her.'

Just when the way seemed closed it opened completely. Within the hour the ritual of the gifting was over and we were heading west to join the circle. There was even time to honour a promise to Alan to visit one of the sacred earth mounds of his people. When we eventually stopped to sleep we had covered over 800 miles in the day.

Day 14. Two days remained to return to Grandfather Titus of the Hopi to complete the circle in 15 days. One stone was still to be gifted but it defied our best efforts to solve its mysteries. We pondered over the clues...

'Hunter of the Quail... a trail... moose at the end of it, laughing, running, fleet of foot... bow... arrow... quiver... javelin thrower... dappled horses... round rings painted on them... shield on left arm, white feathers hanging around it... white feathers on the head of the man.'

Eleven Nations within the 'circle of the dream' now held the stone. This number seemed important, so I let my mind travel with it and let the quest for the twelfth Nation rest. If it was to be, it would be. We were out of time and into timing.

Day 15. We came to Grandfather Titus at his old hut in the corn fields. When we sat with him eleven people were present and when he showed us a Sun symbol he had drawn on the wall it had eleven rays. I do not understand the symbolism but I do know it was very important to him.

My mind had been drifting into the old lore and came to 'eleven posts'. They formed the inner circle of the round houses of the mountain trails. A crucial part of the structure that supported and created the central space where everything was tapu, was of the realm of the gods. The fire that warmed the house was at its centre. This was the sacred nest that sustained the people. Here they gathered to sleep and dream. Had we placed the inner posts of a house of dreams within the heart of this nation? Was the sacred hoop being mended?

What about the twelfth nation? After I left those shores the last stone found its home through Cornelius, Maru and Robert Archer. The riddle solved itself. Coincidence brought Robert Archer to the Zuni, and Hollow Reed, a blonde- haired, blue-green eyed man became its keeper.

I left with the inner circle of eleven stones in place. I like to think the gifting of the twelfth, of itself, created a second circle around the first. The round houses for the trails were built with one circle inside another. The space between them was filled with bundles of raupo reeds to keep out the bitter winds of winter and protect those within.

We were invisible to Grandfather Titus. I sat quietly in a corner while those we didn't know talked lightly of local matters. I wondered if he had forgotten who we were, and if the hours we spent together to open the great circle had slipped from his mind. Was the whole journey empty of meaning? If this old one was no longer part of it, how could the circle be closed?

I kept silent and waited for an hour. Then the other visitors left and Grandfather Titus acknowledged our presence for the first time. He sat on his low bed wearing a tee shirt advertising the 'Hard Rock Cafe California'. Sometimes he looked a hundred and twelve and at other times like a very, small ten year old boy. Wendy had given him a brown double sheep skin rug to sleep on. His excited response was...

'She brings me buffalo. She brings me buffalo.'

This with a smile and deep enjoyment. He was in another world in another time. What a perfect gift. It seems buffalo has something of the feel of wool. No one felt it was necessary to tell him it was anything else. Soon all Hopiland knew the old one rested on a buffalo skin.

Grandfather beckoned Roy to him. They spoke too quietly to be heard by us. Then Roy, who was the old man's nurse, cook, driver and minder, explained he would tell us the story of a journey he made recently...

> 'One day Grandfather asked me to prepare for a journey to copy a sacred picture carved in stone in the mountains. I packed food, sleeping mats and all that would be needed and drove the vehicle to the door.
>
> Grandfather came out but wouldn't climb in. He told me to go alone. To drive down the road and whenever I was unsure of the route to wait and listen.
>
> I drove off with a big roll of paper for the drawing and pieces of charcoal for pencils. And whenever I was uncertain of a turning I stopped, and a 'yes' or 'no' entered my mind, and after a long drive I came to the mountains and left the vehicle.
>
> Trusting Grandfathers 'promptings' I came at last to a long rock wall and this was what was carved into the stone.'

Roy moved over to the large sheet of paper that covered most of the far wall of the little hut. It was probably eight or nine feet long. Before us was the charcoal drawing and on its left side was a great Sun with eleven rays. He took up the story again.

> 'This is the history of the world from the beginning, when we crawled out of the place beneath the earth, until now.'

I was trying to take all this in. Roy pointed to the bottom left corner to show us the beginning and to the top right to indicate now. 'This is where we are today.' As he explained the journey of humanity through the ages I remained mesmerized by the 'now', by where we were today. I began to see in my mind a Shaman of great power sitting before a stone wall and charting across it the ebb and flow of tides that were still to come. I suspected, from the history being shared, that the one who hammered this prophecy into the stone did so thousands of years ago.

Roy continued through the pageant of the past, showed the arrival of the White Man and moved on to wars in recent times and came to today. What transfixed me was that 'now' was the end of the line.

Grandfather spoke...

'There are two paths now.' He pointed to the jagged fork that descended sharply to end abruptly. 'That is a bad trail. There everything will finish. The sacred hoop will break beyond mending. I feared it was to be the one.'

Again and again the old ones on the long trail had spoken of the significance of this age. 'What time is it,' they said. Now, Titus was making it very clear. He pointed again...

'This is the upper trail. It is the trail of the one hearted people, the trail of truth and love.'
Then his voice grew stronger and he said, 'We can win. We are winning. There are enough one hearted people. The evil in the world is devouring itself.'

Titus explained the 'evil' as - those who pollute the land, those who bring sickness to the waters and steal the clear skies, those who rape the earth, the violent ones who kill, and those who are not honest. He smiled. The doubt he showed the day he opened the way for our journey was gone. He was buoyant and wanted us to share that feeling. There was hope.

As the day closed I tried to prepare myself for the parting. I felt Titus and I would not meet again. His age sat heavily upon him and I was soon to cross the ocean to my home so far away.

Grandfather called me to him. He was on a low bench so I sat cross-legged at his feet. Roy appeared and placed a freshly worked piece of wood in the old one's hand. Titus placed this long curved stick in my hands. Then Roy explained...

> 'As soon as you left to travel the circle, Grandfather sent me to get a piece of ocatillo wood. Each day he scraped and shaped it. It is his gift to you. It is the snake stick of the Hopi people, a talking stick of great power. It searches for the truth to bring change and healing. He asks you to carry the snake for the Hopi Nation, and for the families of the people of peace. It is your companion on the trails.'

Then the old one said with great feeling...

> 'Do not be angry! If others send arrows at you, do not be angry. No matter what they say, do not be angry. Do everything with love. Send only love to those who send you pain.'

Our leave taking was very difficult. I knelt before the old one and embraced him and our tears blessed the snake stick. Words were of no moment now and in the end I simply stood up and quietly left. No 'Goodbyes' were said. The door was left open for all the days to come.

Grandfather Titus died in the autumn of 1994. At that time I was on the trail of the ancestors who set the great standing stones in place across the face of Europe. My hope was to see him on the way home. Although that was not to be, he has never been very far from me. His last words to me, when I last saw him in his little hut in the cornfields, were...

> 'Feed the Sun each day. Make smoke and talk to me.'

On returning to New Zealand I put the snake stick in the Kaumatua's hands. He said...

'The old man sends a message. The Snake People come to this land for the first time.'

The tokotoko I carried on so many trails was given again to Waitaha. Thereafter I was to walk with the snake stick. I had some glimmerings of the role of the Snake People. Their arrival was good for all of us. The truth seekers were set free in the land. It was a time of change.

On finishing the circle I sought advice from Indian elders on the way ahead for me. I was told my trail was not to South America. The words were...

'That land is like a reptile devouring its own tail. It writhes in such pain it would kill you, even though you go with love.'

I then asked about the power of the greenstone we placed in the circle of the Twelve Nations...

'The land needs to have its birth substance renewed. Greenstone is the seed, the birthstone. It is time for it to go to all continents and islands.'

When I displayed tiredness at the thought of carrying pounamu to so many places, I was gently told. 'You are more vulnerable than you think. Go home now and rest. Teach others to carry the stone to the world. And when you go to Tibet take younger ones to climb the heights for you.'

Tibet? I was intrigued. What adventures lay ahead?

'What is not of the spirit will not last.
The real world is the world of the spirit.'

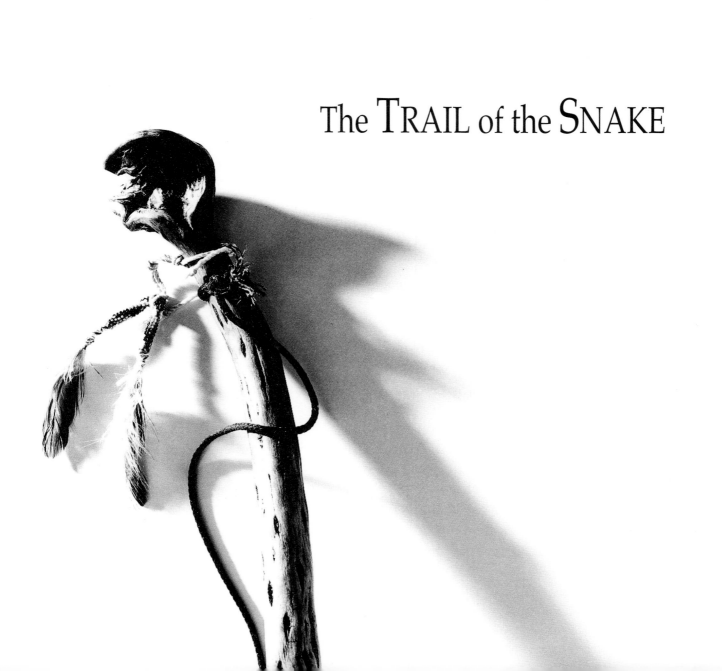

The TRAIL of the SNAKE

THE TRUTH IN THE SHADOWS

'Walk with the snake stick for my people, and many peoples. Walk to test the truth within.'

Grandfather Titus of the Hopi

My greatest teachers on this journey with 'Song of Waitaha' were those who put obstacles in the way. Some were friends who came alongside the waka to help and nearly tipped it over as they clambered aboard. Others were opponents who feared its publication. The latter were few but powerfully placed politically. I owe them much because I grew through the experience and the book gained. Their opposition added depth and richness to the work, delayed its publication by several years and ensured it appeared in the right way at the right time.

When Pani Manawatu set us to the task in 1988, we were bound by our promise to see it through. Only he could lift that from us.

In January 1990 a Kaumatua from the North Island came to my home to read the partly completed manuscript. We talked for hours and the words lay untouched before him. Eventually I asked if he would like to read the text. He gently placed his hand on the pages, closed his eyes and a visible shiver went through his body. He said...

'The wairua is there. I have felt the spirit of the words. It is time to bring the kaupapa to the North. The old families will gather once more.'

In May 1990 Waitaha came together until over 100 tribes were represented on the marae. Overhead four rainbows layered on top of each other against the clouds. Their colours honoured the work and reminded me this was the first wananga of this kind for over fifty years.

It was time for the people of peace to walk in their strength. After five days of discussion the elders stood in turn to say..

'Tautoku. We support the kaupapa to the death,' meaning, 'We open our baskets of knowledge, we give you everything.'

The dream of Pani Manawatu was now carried by the families of Waitaha throughout the land. We joked about those who opposed the work, whoever they might be, marvelled at the length of their tentacles and referred to them as the 'octopus'.

Months later we received a message from Pani Manawatu saying...

'Have faith. The taniwha is about to confront you. Stand firm and at the end of the trail it will be a benevolent one.'

The way ahead was made very clear. When arrows of anger were thrown at me I was asked to reply with gentleness. 'Send only love ' was the instruction I followed and it worked. I did not hit back. I even saved some who led the attacks from public embarrassment on occasions, yet they know nothing of this. Anger and hate did not eat away at me. I remained open and vulnerable. In many ways protected by my innocence.

When I spoke to the elders about this opposition they smiled and said...

'It adds mana to the work. Ruaumoko, the god of earthquakes, shakes us to see if we are able to stand firm. It makes us grow.'

Those who opposed the book were sending a shock wave through the world of Waitaha. It challenged the people to look to their strength, to stand tall and honour the ancestors. It was in that spirit that Dame Whina Cooper came to Wellington to support a funding application. We didn't get the financial assistance requested. The octopus seemed to be ever present and making life difficult. Those who opposed and those who helped the book all worked in their frailty, with blind spots and blemishes that led to error. I was learning to walk the shadows and see the shadow and the light are of the same source. As a friend said...

'Without our shadow we are nothing. If our shadow leaves us, we die.'

It was time to find another way to fund the printing. Two trails converged to provide the key. The first was marked by fire and the second by stone. It began when I remembered the words of the Kuia who freed me of the need to light the trail fires to greet the dawn. She said...

'The fires are not needed now. Every word you write is a flame.'

Then I realised you cannot light a fire by holding a match to a big log. This fire would be lit by gathering many twigs together. We would get the book to the people by going to the people. To thousands who would each contribute a little fuel to light the flame. I began with a list of 200 names and discovered each carried pounamu I had given to them in recent years.

All were sent several small, beautifully crafted brochures and asked to spread the word. We needed people to buy the book sight unseen, months ahead of publication. It was to be an act of trust. The first fliers went out in Christchurch and within weeks, orders arrived from most cities in New Zealand and from Australia, Canada, the USA and Britain.

In March I took to the road to tell the story of Waitaha in people's homes. There were no public meetings. Back and forwards I went through the North and South Islands. Sometimes half a dozen people were there and sometimes twenty or thirty. The book moved on trust and in the old way with people talking and sharing their vision and excitement.

Meanwhile, behind the scenes craftsmen were working on the treasure box to hold the leather bound edition of 'Song of Waitaha'. It was inlaid with pounamu and whalebone. We were committed to producing five hundred and twenty five copies.

We went to the Ngatihine Forest Trust to ask for kauri, the rarest of the timbers. They responded by saying they were 'honoured to be asked'. The people decided to gift a standing kauri to the book. They had not cut such a tree for 80 years, so this was a great sacrifice for the work. I was asked to choose the tree and went to the tallest and truest to honour the mana of Taane. To thank Ngatihine I wrote a story to give to their children to commemorate this day...

> 'The people gathered from the Four Winds, from many wonderful places beneath the brightest stars of Aotearoa. They came to honour the tree that would fall that day. Its name was 'Kauri'.
>
> They went to the forest where Kauri stood so tall and true. Old people, young people, those who walked with wisdom and those who sought wisdom. All gathered in the bright Sun to be with the Kaumatua who stood before the forest to ask Taane Mahuta for one of his tall children... the one named Kauri.
>
> With gentleness and love born of ancestors bound within the tides of time, the Kaumatua spoke thus to Kauri...

> > 'Great and wondrous Kauri so tall and true,
> > we stand before you to ask for the gift of your life.
> > We ask this for our children and all the children beneath
> > the stars, for they need a waka of great mana to carry their
> > dreams into tomorrow and all their tomorrows.'

These words were spoken and many more besides. In the silence that followed the karakia the winds moved with sudden power to shake the tallest branches of Kauri. The birds joined as one to sing their sweetest songs. And riroriro sang the words that called the ancestors to the stone trails and the long tides.

All who gathered there, the old and the young, knew the tree understood their need and offered its life to the sweeping blades. When the moment came for the last blow to fall, it swept in cleanly. A great sigh echoed through the trunk to reach the stars beyond the Sun. And Kauri slowly leaned towards the Earth Mother and fell into her arms.

Silence. Silence in the land. Silence within our being. All was bound together in Silence.

Then joy leapt forth with birdsong. Tears ran to touch lips. Their salt taste opened memories of the ocean, and the sea trails that gathered our people to this land. We saw again the great waka that sailed the long tides. And we saw the dreams of old reawakening in the world.

Remember that, when the wisdom of the ancestors walks the land again.

Remember that, when you go to honour the fifteen kauri planted to replace the one that fell.

Remember that, when the wind touches the tops of the trees and the birds join as one to sing of the wonderful days to come.

Remember Kauri.'

The rarest of the woods for the Special Edition was soon to be on the waters and bound for Christchurch. The greenstone to be inlaid in the kauri lid of the treasure box was being cut by Clem Mellish, a very fine carver. The engraving for embossing the leather cover with the tuatara design was already completed by Robert Hiseman, one of the last great craftsmen in his field. It was an exquisite gift to the children of the land that was now his home.

In these ways, and many more, everything was moving strongly towards publication. There was great rejoicing when Derek Lardelli, the creator of the superb illustrations, finally got the face of the 'Orator' to appear. This powerful figure, who opens each chapter and carries the words through every page, was reluctant to reveal his image until the last words had been written. When the elders saw Derek's work they said...

'He has stepped back two thousand years to take us a thousand years into the future'

All who came close to the book were challenged to find the truth within themselves. Magnificent work was done by those who gathered to help bring this great waka of dreams safely home. Even those who opposed it played their part. Obstacles gave birth to opportunities. There was healing on the trail of the snake.

Greenstone was being carried to Africa, South America, Asia, Central America, Europe and Australia. The cry of the American Indian elders was being answered. Now the stone was singing to me. I needed to journey to ancient worlds where sentinels of rock stood tall to greet the stars. They called me home to ancestors across the widest of oceans to meet the timeless ones.

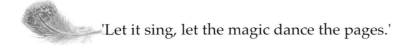'Let it sing, let the magic dance the pages.'

The TRAIL of the TUATARA

IN THE LANDS OF THE STANDING STONES

'Listen to the sacred spirit of the winds, the voices of the old ones long gone from us.'

The spirit of the old one, the tuatara, guides us on this trail. This wonderful creature, born of the age of the dinosaurs, opens the way to the most ancient of knowledge. Its third eye, now hidden from most of us, sees into realms that join with the stars. When we think of tuatara we remember our dead, those now gone from us but ever present in memory. For when the spirit departs this world it passes tuatara on its way to the stars from whence it came.

During the years of the journey with the book we lost many elders to the tides of time. Pani Manawatu, Renata Kauere, Frank McDonald, Patariki Te Rei, Marie Te Maiharoa, George Ruka and many others left us before the work was done. Each has a story to be told for they were all part of the dream. May the story of two, speak for the dedication of the many.

Dame Whina Cooper died in March, 1994. She first came to stand alongside 'Song of Waitaha' in October 1990 when she travelled to Wellington to the Wakapuwahia Marae, Porirua. There she joined many elders, who came from the four winds, to support an application for funding to print the book.

Auntie Whina made the long journey by car from Hokianga with Eddie Kawiti, her gentle nurse and companion. Sitting in her wheelchair she spoke for two hours on the marae, telling us of her support for sharing the old knowledge and of her dreams for the children of this land.

She asked to see the book completed for her to hold before she died. As she was ninety-two when she made that request I wondered if there would be enough time left to meet her wish. Yet I was aware that in her own way she had issued a challenge, set in place an urgency, I felt committed to meet.

In the years that followed the 1990 meeting she talked often of her book that was still to come, and how she was waiting for it. Some of the media people mistakenly thought she meant a book about herself but she was looking with eyes fixed on other horizons.

In November 1993 I spent two weeks making a copy of 'Song of Waitaha' by hand. All the illustrations and maps were colour copied from the originals and pasted into the text and everything was bound within the leather embossed cover adorned with the tuatara carving. Then it was wrapped in handmade harakeke paper and placed in a wakahuia, a treasure box made of kauri, totara and kahikatea and inlaid with whalebone and pounamu. It was ready and waited on Whina's call for it to travel.

It wasn't until Monday 21st, March 1994 that she sent a message to the elders to say...

'I am going soon. I am more in the other world than this one. It is time to bring the book.'

Thursday 24th. When Auntie Whina knew 'Song of Waitaha' was on its way she discharged herself from Middlemore Hospital at four o'clock in the morning. She was going home to Panguru to die.

Friday 25th. The book was carried to her bedside at midnight. The Moon had reached its fullness; it was the time of her leaving. During that evening some thought she was drifting off to realms from which she would not return, but she had waited too long to be denied her wish to hold the story of the ancestors close before she departed. She stirred. Her eyes cleared. The wairua of the taonga called to her, the pages were opened and she filled her world with them for the next two hours. And she blessed the sacred writings.

At two o'clock in the morning the book began another journey. It was taken through the night to Wellington to be with Patariki Te Rei. This gentle chief of great standing spent the afternoon quietly turning its pages, but mostly waiting. Late in the afternoon he quietly said...

'She has gone. The old one has left us.'

Then Patariki Te Rei took up his pen and began to write the words to close the book. He was the keeper of karakia entrusted to very few, and had already decided to use the first twelve lines of one of the most ancient prayers. Yet when they were written he paused and, instead of putting down his pen, he smiled and continued to write, sharing with the world line after line of that prayer until it filled three pages.

The circle closed. The way was opened for 'Song of Waitaha' to be printed and placed in the hands of the people. Yet there was more to come. Dame Whina Cooper had asked that her last message to the nation be bound within the pages. It is there for all to cherish. A wonderful call to us to live together with mutual respect and understanding, to live in peace, to remember the ancestors who sailed from many lands to call this land home.

My last great trail took me around the world to honour ancestors far beyond these shores. It led to the standing stones of the ancients, to the megalithic sites of western Europe, sacred stone altars to the spirit, built long before the pyramids of Egypt. The way home was through North America, Hawaii and Australia.

Kaylynn Two Trees played a role in the shaping of this journey. She invited me to begin this book in her land, with the Lakota, and others who gathered to walk a new dream. Pine Ridge, in Dakota, was her home village and she was building another in New Mexico. Kaylynn worked to see the birthing of the New Nation that brought all peoples together in peace.

Initially my plan was just to go to North America. Then an invitation arrived for me to assist a team writing a history of the maps of the peoples of the world. They hoped I could write about Pacific maps with Waitaha navigation charts and trail maps in mind. This project would take me to work with Malcolm Lewis in the University of Sheffield, David Woodward and Peter Nabokov in the University of Wisconsin and Ben Finney in the University of Hawaii. The most economical way to fly was on a 'Global Explorer' ticket. That sounded perfect.

A huge trail was opening up. I now reflected on words Rose Pere shared earlier that year. This wise woman, who helps and inspires so many, said...

> 'The spirit of 'Song of Waitaha' goes deep within this land. It reaches back to my ancestors, then travels far beyond these shores to times long forgotten and comes at last to Glastonbury.'

When the Sheffield University connection fell so neatly into place, her words marked the way. In her home at Lake Waikaremoana Rose completed the shape of the journey by saying I was to carry a very special piece of pounamu with me. It was a gift from Geoff Robson, a fisherman in South Westland. Its true colour and depth was only revealed when I worked its surface with my hands to wear away the grey outer covering of age. Rose said...

> 'Open the way as you go through the land. You know what I mean. And remember this beautiful pounamu is your guide and the key to the doors along the trail.'

The day I left New Zealand for London I heard that Kaylynn's art project in Miami was now behind schedule and our arrangement to be in her village could not be met. I was disappointed. Part of me had really looked forward to spending some time in a tepee surrounded by snow. Although it was not to be at this time, it had set in place the journey around the world carrying an eighteen pound (8 kilogramme) stone, plus many of its smaller brothers and sisters.

The 'Global Explorer' flight in September 1994, took me away with the book still unpublished. Printing delays caused that to happen. There was huge pressure to stay for the launching but I felt the pull of this trail. I knew my work with 'Song of Waitaha' was done. I had raised the money. Tom would see the printing through in his careful way, the elders would carry it on to the marae, and the people would walk with their story again. It was time for me to let it go. The book belonged to Waitaha. It was theirs to launch on the new tides.

Many ancient places called me home. I had not been to Britain before and came to honour my own family, ancestors with roots deep within these isles. In the Derbyshire section of the Domesday Book, compiled in 1086, the entry for the village of Brailsford reads... 'Elfin holds it.' The entries for Bupton, nearby, and Osmaston a few miles hence, have the same words. Elfin's son, Nicholas, was surnamed de Brailsford. The family appears to be of Saxon descent, athough there is also a case for it being Celtic in origin. Whatever the line, I remain delighted with my descent from great, grandfather Elfin.

The elfin trail led first to Scotland, to Mull and the Island of Iona. The how and where of that journey was found very quickly by simply riding the lift in the YMCA hostel in Glasgow for ten minutes. Each time the doors opened and someone stepped in, there was another source of information. Everything fell into place very easily and the next evening I stood on the bleak and beautiful shores of Mull looking at Iona.

The dawn ferry to Iona brought me into a world of ancestral power. The ancient kings of Ireland, Scotland and Norway lay buried here. Celtic carving still endured in the stone and the spirit of the old ones lingered on. I came because the 'Book of Kells', the most famous of all the Medieval illuminated manuscripts, began its life here. Some 1200 years ago Celtic monks spent countless hours penning the four Gospels beneath these open skies. Modern analysis reveals the brilliantly coloured inks came from throughout Europe and as far away as Afghanistan. Each page was illustrated with symbols of the ancient way. Animals, intricate signs and beautiful designs melded the message of the Christ with the power of the sacred images of the Celts and Druids. Great tides met on those pages to carry the dream of peace and love to that age and beyond.

My mother's name was Kells. It was strange 'Song of Waitaha' also carried the ancient message of the people of peace into the world. The sacred words, once held only in the songs of the wisdomkeepers, were soon to be shared.

Drawn here by these parallells, I came to this island and found there a spirit of overwhelming peace. I carried greenstone to leave with those dedicated to the restoration of the Iona Abbey. My plan was to spend the night on the island but that came to nought. As I diligently sought someone to care for the stone, I came to shut doors and notices saying, 'Please do not disturb... Meeting in progress.' Three times this happened. Eventually I opened one of those doors to find five people sitting around a table. Before I could say a word, I was politely told they were busy and asked to leave. The stone was clearly not to stay here. I left on the noon ferry. Someone, or something, was calling me back to Mull.

One of the grandmothers met me soon after I left the ferry. Her daughter had told her I was asking about standing stones. She had that knowledge. Following her map I went with one piece of pounamu, the stone I'd taken to Iona. I found a tall stone standing alone high on the slope of a grassed field. The power of this ancient sentinel reached out in all directions. It rose some eight or nine feet to look out on a wide sweep of coastline and many small islands.

I went and said who I was and told the story of my journey. Then I took from my pack the small pounamu and was amazed. The tall standing stone and the small greenstone were the same shape. I held a replica of the standing stone in my hand. Any of a dozen stones in my bag might have come to this place but I chose this one. No! It chose itself.

Leaving the pounamu beside the tall one, I sat in the Sun. My eyes drifted over a free, wild expanse of beauty. Out of the stillness of this land a thought surfaced from the deeps. This standing stone was not placed here in its aloneness to sing just to these fields. Perhaps its voice joined with other sentinels.

If the words I shared with this stone echoed far beyond here, that changed the way the trails might be walked. I saw that by honouring one sacred marker in each land I might be honouring all within its borders. Words given to one opened the way to others. Time spent talking and listening in one special place could sometimes be the whole journey. That helped me understand my need to spend hours in one place, to have the space to sit and rest, to breathe, to hear the sounds, to listen to the music of the land and to sleep awhile.

A storm approached. It was time to go. I intended to leave the pounamu beside the standing stone. However, as I said my farewells a very clear thought came to me. I don't hear voices, just listen to what comes into my mind and trust that first sound image. 'Take the stone. It does not stay.' was the picture. 'Go with it now and do not look back.' Walking away I remembered another thought that came when I'd earlier tried to leave a stone in a forest in Holland. It did not stay either. The land would now be healed by people and stone, not stone on its own. We needed the land and the land needed us. People have the spirit of nurture within them. That was the message behind Bear Claw's instructions to me for the journey to form the great circle of the Twelve Nations...

> 'When you come to the tall trees, the grandfathers and grandmothers, assure them there will be a place in the world for their children.'

That wonderful piece of pounamu I'd tried to leave at Iona and the standing stone, stayed with me until ten minutes before I left Scotland. I was convinced it was going home to New Zealand. Then, I accidentally met a Scotswoman who was of the old wisdom. Diane MacDonald had degrees in law, psychology and anthropology. Her masters thesis in anthropology was on the ancient lore of her people, the old ones of Mull. That beautiful island was her home. She was indeed the one chosen by the stone.

I hastily placed the stone in Diane's hand as a taxi arrived. She held me very close. She immediately understood and later wrote to say it had been named 'Cairngorm'. One day we will meet to share its story.

My trail was now to York and the Minster. I sat for hours taking in the power of this cathedral's soaring stone - giving thanks for the genius of the minds that brought such beauty to the world, and to the roughened hands that shaped the stone to set the spirit of the columns free. It was a warm day but a coldness came over me. I shivered and felt the need for additional clothing. I just had to buy a soft wool jersey to wear against my skin. In the fitting room of the shop I stripped off my shirt and gasped at my bared chest. A vivid ragged red mark the size of a closed fist sat over my heart. A few smaller splashes of red appeared beyond it. Nearly a year later it is still there, a little smaller now and faded to a dull brown. It remains a mystery - a birth mark for this trail.

Ireland called me home. It is indeed the land of the standing stones. There are something like 600 megalithic sites in Europe and 400 of them are in that fair isle. I knew ahead of time the places I wanted to see. To my great joy and amusement my rental car was a beautiful little Renault 'Elf'.

The Rath of Tara, was visited at dawn. Some see it as the birthplace of the spirit of Ireland. At its centre is the 'Stone of Destiny' a beautiful obelisk with a warm heart. It radiated gentleness, nurture and caring on a bleak morning cut by a very cold wind. I carefully placed everything I carried for the sacredness of the journey beside it. All the stones and feathers, the snake stick and the water. Then I lay in the shelter of the giant circle hollowed into the hill. It surrounded the Stone and provided a lovely place to sleep for awhile.

New Grange one of the greatest of the old stone structures is now so popular some have to wait for hours to enter. I went after visiting the Rath of Tara at the opening of the gates and stood with half a dozen who waited on the guide. This dome of fitted stones covers more than two acres and is older than the pyramids. Everywhere I looked the carved surfaces of the large foundation stones revealed images seen in the Anasazi sites of Colorado and Utah and Waitaha in New Zealand. The large pounamu I was carrying to the sacred places of the ancestors sang to the spirals carved deep in the rock.

We walked the tunnel that took us into the heart of New Grange. The inner chamber was unique, unlike anything I had ever experienced. There was great calmness here and learning. Carved symbols on the walls emphasised the reverence that filled this space. Alcoves shaped to fill the mind with balance, housed immense, immaculately dished stone bowls. It is named a burial chamber but everything I saw said it was more. This was a hall for the living. Each year, on December 22, when the dawn sky is clear of cloud, the Sun enters this chamber through a small window and sends a narrow shaft of light into its very heart. Light is life. The shallow bowls so beautifully shaped call out for water not bones. Cleansing waters and the dedication of youth come to mind. It was not hard to imagine young men and women gathered here to learn the ancient lore.

Five lingered in that chamber. Little was said. The guide seemed happy to give us time to listen, to experience the depths of this wondrous place. Then the time arrived to send old words to echo along these walls. I asked if they would like to hear a little of my story. When it was told, I invited them to join me for the karakia to honour the ancient stone trails. The huge pounamu was taken out of its woven basket of flax and placed upon the earth and we formed a circle about it. Water from Waikoropupu, in Takaka, was sprinkled on the greenstone, the snake stick was taken up and I chanted the old words.

No one spoke. We left in silence. I felt the words so ancient and powerful had come home. This was an ageless and sacred dome of stone.

Refreshed I gathered in my treasures and drove to Northern Ireland to close a circle that began on the West Coast of New Zealand several years ago. Dympna McNeice, who walked with me to the sacred waters in Nelson, lived at Portadown, in the 'murder triangle' of that troubled land. Thirteen children were raised in their stone cottage that sat so strongly on their few acres of land. Cattle and a small coal delivery business brought in their food and courage warmed the home.

They were part of a Roman Catholic minority within a strong Protestant territory. Gunfire, frequent helicopter overflights, security sweeps by British troops, rifle fire, and explosions on the roads and in the towns were all part of daily life in the times they simply described as 'The Troubles'. The centre of Portadown still awaited rebuilding following a bombing in the previous year.

Three weeks earlier Dympna's father had died of an illness. It was a sudden loss and the family were still adjusting. Yet a wonderful Kiwi meal with fish, sausages, chips, pavlova, chocolate cake and tea was waiting when I arrived. Dympna and the family were determined to make me feel at home. I knew this was where I would leave the pounamu for Ireland. It was October 1994 and the Peace seemed to be holding. There was hope in the air. My karakia was said for healing and life, for the children of all who called this country home.

Ireland was a revelation. A beautiful countryside of green pastures, stone walls, copses of autumn coloured trees, winding country lanes, warm hearted people and wondrous standing stones. My trail ran to Carrowmore, with its great stone circles and lintels and Creevykeel, a placed of mystery and power. Then on to the Burren, a magical landscape that filled me with awe. There the heart stone of the earth was bared to the skies. A great hand had scraped away the soils to reveal limestone beautifully carved by ancient waters.

The little village of Killaloe, in County Clare, sat beside the River Shannon and held within St Flannans Cathedral a wonderful carved stone. It was found in 1916, deep within one of the walls surrounding the cemetery, having been buried there for many centuries. This stones's beauty was not in fine carving, because it had none, but in the words cut deep into its surface. It was the base of a cross shaft, the broken stump of a tall Christian Cross. The words were carved there by a Christian Norseman, who had sweated over this hard stone, wielding his hammer a thousand years ago. It is the only stone in Ireland bearing a complete inscription in Runes and Celtic Oghams.

Translated the Runes said... THORGRIMR CARVED THIS CROSS

Then in another hand, and the blows of another's hammer, these words in another language...

A BLESSING UPON THORGRIMR

The power of this remnant of the past reached into me. My heart went to Thorgrimr, whose cross is gone, broken by chance or vengeance, but whose words linger on. Revealed for all to see after centuries of entombment in a high stone wall. One of the Stone People had reached across the ages to say we all carve our story. Some in stone, others in the land, or in the lives of those we meet along the way. The words 'Thorgrimr carved this cross' seemed to sum up a life. And those of the other hand that spelt out, 'A blessing upon Thorgrimr,' speak of respect and love, of one offering nurture to another.

This stone was a crossroad, a meeting of peoples and a symbol of the way the world might be. Once again the great pounamu I carried from my home had guided me into the realms of the old ones who honoured the stone and the Great Spirit.

It was hard to leave Ireland and journey on to England. However, Glastonbury and Stonehenge called with their own special songs, and as I listened I thought often of the standing stone on Mull. Did it follow my journey and share the story of the stone?

Sherwood Forest was my next destination. It was time to see Malcolm Lewis, of Sheffield University. This extraordinary man was captured by the spirit of American Indian maps early in his career. He tells the story as if he is still a little bemused by it all. I am not at all surprised his life's work took that direction. A greater keeper of such treasures is hard to imagine. He is a world authority who thrills to the markers of the ancient trails. We walked in the nearby remnants of the ancient Forest of Sherwood. He talked of his work. It was a joy to share this time with him and his wife Margaret. In the evening I told some of the stories of the stone trails and knew she was to be the keeper of the pounamu I was to leave in England. After the karakia for the stone I left. This was a wonderful place for it to sing.

Glastonbury Tor was climbed as the Sun was setting amidst brilliant slanting rays of rainbow light. The large pounamu made the journey up the steep slope, and another large stone still wrapped in the cloth that covered it for the journey. It came from a river within the central mountain basins of the South Island of New Zealand and was dedicated to the spirit of this land. The request was for it to be buried on Glastonbury Tor, but I came without a shovel or a plan.

On the gentle slope to the west of the Saint Michael Tower I found a perfectly constructed place to house this treasure. It was an abandoned mole hole. As I wanted to gift this stone within a circle of people I went to a young woman who was meditating nearby and invited her to join me. Then I asked a family sitting in the shelter. They brought other friends so we numbered fifteen. There were five children aged from two to seven. They unwrapped the stone together. Everyone somehow 'helped' with even the smallest one being given a place. The stone was then passed around the circle until it came again into the hands of the young ones. They carried it to the hole and placed it carefully within. Water was scattered over this pure white stone, the karakia was said and everyone brought handfuls of soil from mole mounds nearby to cover it.

Catherine, who gathered the stone and sent it on its way, would be pleased to know it was in the earth. Rose Pere's words, spoken in New Zealand to tie 'Song of Waitaha' to Glastonbury, returned to say another circle was joined.

Stonehenge was a difficult experience for me. The moment I emerged from the access walkway under the road I was troubled. Thinking back it began several hours earlier. Soon after I left Glastonbury I saw a badger lying on a narrow country road. It had few visible injuries but was dead. I carried it into a nearby forest and came to what I thought was its home. I found a place to leave it. Thoughts of the badger went with me to Stonehenge.

Stonehenge called to the depths of me. There was power here and pain. This sacred altar of stone, this awesome circle of ancient knowledge, was surrounded and separated by roads. A busy arterial highway cut between the central circle and the line of sentinels that radiated out from it. The M3 motorway curved across on the other side. The noise was overwhelming. I sat on the grass outside the low barrier that isolated me from the stones and used earplugs to try to find a quieter place. I failed.

Then I stepped over the barrier to walk the line inside the fence beside the road. I wanted to take water from a spring in Ireland to the outlying stone 50 metres from the circle. Halfway there whistles began to blow. Guards began to run. I was in trouble. And so was Stonehenge.

Two things comforted me as I left. The authorities didn't know a piece of pounamu already lay buried in the centre of the great circle. Waitaha took it there in the gathering darkness not long ago to honour the ancestors and begin the healing. Secondly, where I couldn't go I had sent my thoughts and prayers; a badger waited there to take them to the stone.

On the journey back to New Zealand there were friends to see and commitments to universities, but no standing stones to greet. That part of the trail was completed.

The flight from Britain to the United States crossed the trails of the whales. These wide Atlantic waters were a barrier to some and a highway to others. I was not surprised to discover the Ojibwa of Garden River, Canada, knew I was travelling with a stone for them, even though I had not been in touch for a year. When I phoned Willard Pine from Milwaukee he said...

'We expected to hear from you today. You were there when we made the smoke this morning. The stone will help us. When can you come?'

The 'moccasin telegraph' was still working perfectly by the light of the fire. Unfortunately transport from Milwaukee to Sault Sainte Marie was not as fast. I found I could not take the stone myself and still meet my commitments to the university. When that door shut for me, it opened for another. Ros Woodward, the wife of the professor I was working with at Wisconsin University, was closely joined with the Indian Nations in many ways. Before I left for Europe she sent me a beautiful Indian 'dreamcatcher'. It was to be her journey to the Ojibwa with the stone in the spring, her trail, and her dream that was to be woven into the tapestry. She also became the keeper of the stone I left for North America. It was dedicated to honour the wisdom held within the sacred charts and maps of the ancients.

I was inspired by the work of the scholars who were preserving for all time the maps of the great trail makers of the past. The sacred treasures of all peoples were being honoured in this way. It was wonderful to share their vision and to be able to gift pounamu to the seven in the team and a whale's tooth to their leader, David Woodward. Their final work on the maps and charts of the Pacific peoples was about to begin. It was a moving moment for me, when I said the karakia and opened the way for knowledge that would honour the voyages of the old navigators.

Their minds joined star to star to chart the way over the wide oceans. In ancient days other minds reached across time to see the trail ahead and leave prophecies with the people. A white buffalo calf was born while I was in Milwaukee and made me think of the prophecy of the Time of the White Buffalo. The old ones of the Indian Nations spoke of the age when white children would walk with red in their hearts to bring harmony to the world. The spirit of the ancestors would be born again in them. They would learn to trust their dreams and move with one heart to heal the Earth Mother. They would be the Warriors of the Rainbow.

My last journey in North America was to the heights of the Sierra Nevada Mountains not far from Lake Tahoe. The guiding pounamu, that sang to the trails that circled the earth, was carried to the skyline at over 10,000 feet and left deep in the snows for days. I don't know why this was necessary, but I do know the stone changed in appearance during that time. It opened its heart. It had greater translucence. I could see deeper into its core.

In Hawaii, Professor Ben Finney helped me see history in the making. For years he had been closely involved in the development of the sailing programme that took the Hawaiian navigators to the long trails of the ocean again. It was wonderful to see Hukulea at its moorings and stand beside other great waka being prepared for long voyages made solely with the guidance of the ancient lore of the winds, the tides, the currents and the stars. In Hawaii I also saw the green flash on the horizon. That wondrous moment when the setting Sun signals a last farewell. The stone was going home. This trail was closing fast.

'As the pulse of the universe calls so we dance.'

ALL TRAILS LEAD TO KNOWLEDGE

'You open many doors for people.
You are a doorway.'

So I come now to the end of the five trails and my thoughts turn to my family. Barbara has not heard these stories nor have my children. Although they have been part of them we have not been in the space to share deeper things in recent years. There was too much pain there and little understanding of how to talk to each other. We were afraid of the truth, the risk involved in confronting the reality of the paths we walked. We finally separated in December 1994.

When I left for Europe in September Barbara didn't know I might not be returning to her. It seemed wrong to suggest that when I wasn't sure. I couldn't raise that question then disappear for three months. We had parted for a while in 1993. On coming together again we found a new level of understanding, a place where we were more comfortable about sharing our thoughts and feelings. I still loved her and still do. That never changes.

As I had travelled throughout New Zealand to tell the story of Waitaha and gather funds for the printing, I began to realise there were hard choices ahead. I lived in a beautiful house, was comfortable, secure and cared for with consideration and love. Yet, deep down I was lonely to the point of despair. So much ran through the depths of me, the excitement of the journeys, the mystery, the pain, the uncertainty and it could not be shared. A canyon cut through my family life and I felt I was alone on the other side.

There was no blame in this. Each of us makes our own journey following the truth of the moment. I was walking the mystery of old knowledge with peoples who said, 'The real world is the world of the spirit.' I chose this path. Others chose to walk the truth of theirs.

The Song of Waitaha had asked so much of us. I was not the person who began the work in 1988. One friend said, 'You write the book and the book writes you.' My commitment to Waitaha was widening the cracks in the home. There were times when I felt it was all too much and wanted to be free of the dream, to let it die. Yet I could not. Promises had been made and the financial burdens wrapped on our house could only be met by publication. I was just holding on, hoping to finish the work and mend the broken pieces.

I had found a companion who wanted to share the journeys. When I told my Maori sister I had met Cushla and she brought something special into my life, she said...

'Understand that you called her to you. You called her and she came.'

This confused me. How could I call Cushla to me when I hadn't heard from her for 27 years? Whatever the answer, the reality is that she came to support me. This relationship was not about another woman, but about another life and another world.

We 'die' many times in one lifetime. Leaving one place, grieving for the losses, being more alive in the next. That's how I feel when I walk the mountain tops but there are still days when I fall into swamp lands in the darker valleys. That's when I question the cost of the journey with 'Song of Waitaha' and cry in the pain of the sunset of a wonderful marriage. My dream is that the sunset heralds the sunrise, the beginning of a new dream for all of us. A time of continuing friendship. A new journey on a new trail.

Grandchildren carry the dream forward. I said at the beginning I wrote this story to find healing and direction for my life. That has been the way of it. Wynona spoke the truth when she mapped the journey for me. I know the time of secrets is over. I have stepped out a long way to honour that truth. Much of what I reveal of my inner feelings is shared for the first time. I have decided how much to tell. I take responsibility for the words I set free on this trail.

Some things I still hold deep within my heart. That knowledge will be shared with my family and my grandchildren if they wish to walk with it. I know my children bring great gifts to the world. Rodney is a keeper of the gardens, Gordon travels the paths of the waters and the rainbows, Anne is of the magic of the mother and the guide, and Peter brings great teaching to the mountains and to life.

More recently my journey has been shared with another family where Amy brings healing to the sick, Tamzin writes beautiful poetry and stories and Ewan thinks he will be a toymaker. All are joined by the circle of the dream.

There was a time when I thought the only ones who would see this book would be Russell, Andrew, Jeremy and little Kaitlyn, my grandchildren. The thought was to write it for them alone. Now I know I am to share it with your children and your grandchildren, with Desiree, Josef, Michael, Dillon, Rowan, Sam, Madison, Joachim, Mihiata, Te Ahi and any other names you wish to add. There is great magic in this generation. Some treasures are best given into the hands of our grandchildren. They are the seed.They are closest to the magic of life and embrace the wisdom of old with innocence and joy. They are still free to dance with the leprechauns.

A wonderful spirit moves in the world today. Wherever I travel I find people of all ages who are walking the magic. Great changes are taking place around us. It is an exciting time to be really alive. To be ourselves.

It is an age when ordinary people are being asked to do extra-ordinary things, to reach beyond themselves. And they are. The magic is everywhere. It is bound in the courage of young mothers and fathers raising families on their own, having found the strength to leave homes of violence. It moves in the quest of young men and women in prisons who are searching for their trail. It travels in older women and men, who are bravely changing relationships that died many years ago, to make another life. It runs in strong men who attend anger management sessions to learn to heal a hurt buried deep within their lives. It rests in those who triumph by merely finding the energy to get through this day. It stands tall in those who are leaving jobs that no longer make sense to them, and risk insecurity to follow a deeper need. They all seem to be saying... It is time to get a life. To know myself. To be true to myself.

They make their dream, and walk it, and it happens.
They have a life and it is filled with magic.

When I returned to New Zealand in December, after carrying the pounamu to the standing stones, and travelling the great circle of the globe, I found 'Song of Waitaha' had met further delays and was to be launched in two days time. I had made my journey and was back in time to lay the pounamu on the marae. I joined the Waitaha families gathered in Takaka to honour their ancestors and gift the sacred teachings to the world. It was their waka to send on the tides. It always had been. My work was done.

Ko, my sister, and guide through many swamps, thought overwise. She wrote to say...

'I hardly think your involvement is over. This, dear brother is only the beginning. There are other and very important things yet to be done. Admittedly the trails have been extraordinarily difficult, hard, time consuming, great obstacles have been heaved into the paths that were chosen by us, almost unhinging us. We are all in this together. We cannot and should not leave things dangling.

The wonderful taonga 'Song of Waitaha' is a signal for the rest of the Nation of Waitahanui to reawaken and be counted. They need people like yourself to lead them into maturity and understanding, as well, there will be those who need to be led back into the philosophies and truth of the ancient ones. We need you, they need you.'

On the last day of the gathering to launch the book on the marae, the Kaumatua spoke of my future role. He surprised the people by saying...

'Barry is not to speak again on the marae of this land. He has gone to the world on the ancient trails once travelled by Tamatea Pokai Whenua. His marae is now the world. He speaks for Waitaha beyond these shores. He speaks to Waitahanui, the peace nations of the world.'

The words Ko had written were echoed in the Kaumatua's statement. Other trails awaited me beyond these shores. He finished by saying...

'Welcome home Tamatea Pokai Whenua.'

There is no beginning and no end. We turn within the circle. Remember how I had asked Wynona, the medicine woman, if the story of the journey to create the circle of stone in North America should be written. She had replied...

'Yes! And you must write it. But it's not the book you have already planned in your head.'

These are the notes I wrote in my diary that day in July of 1992.

'It is your story that is to be told... tell the story of your many journeys... the story of the spirit... then the pains and the hurt will go... tell your story to understand and be healed.'

This I have shared already, but there was more. Yesterday I turned to the next page of that diary and found words I hadn't seen in the last three years. It was wonderful to read them as I write the last words for these pages. You see, those notes contained the perfect blueprint for this book. Wynona had set it out in detail, and without looking back to her words, it had been followed in a remarkable way...

'It's not a disaster book... not about catastrophes that may befall... it's your personal odyssey... your search for identity in the world... it's about hope... above all it is about hope...

Begin it with the Greenstone Trail... follow the question, Who am I? ... use what some call 'flash backs'... dance around... shift in time... write about yourself... your heart...you are born for something... to give by receiving...

Reveal what you feel safe with revealing... tell stories... be the story teller to the outer world... talk to the friendly faces... they will come expecting to feel...

The elders reveal your role... you are born to find the common ground... reconcile the tribes... harmonise... write and communicate... bring learning... you are the mystical warrior.'

'Some are born of the dreamtime and make their world. Others are born of the world and make their dreams.'

Who am I?

GLOSSARY

Aroha: love
Awhi: warm support

Iwi: tribe

Kai Arahi: trail guide
Karakia: prayer
Kaumatua: male tribal elder
Kaupapa: dream to be achieved
Kete: woven basket
Karowai: cloak
Kuia: female tribal elder
Kumara: sweet potato

Mana: personal standing
Marae: tribal meeting place
Mauri: physical appearance
Mauri ora: life

Noa: the realms of people

Pae Arahi: master of the trails
Pounamu: nephrite, jade, greenstone

Riroriro: grey warbler
Rongo Marae Roa: God of Peace
Ruaumoko: God of Earthquakes

Taane Mahuta: God of Trees & Birds
Taane Nui a Rangi: God of Life
Taniwha: guardian of the waters and land
Taonga: a sacred treasure
Tapu: of the realms of the Gods
Tawhiri Matea: God of the Winds
Tohi: dedication and initiation ceremony
Tohunga: wisdomkeeper
Tokotoko: the talking stick
Tuahu: sacred marked place
Tu Mata Uenga: God of War
Tuatara: lizard like reptile

Waiata: song, record of the past
Wairua: the spirit, that which continues
Waka: ocean going vessel, a canoe
Whare Wananga: School of Learning

ACKNOWLEDGEMENTS

In honouring the mountains, rivers and lands where these words were written with so much nurture, I give thanks to Dame Te Atairangikaahu and the people of Tainui.

My sincere thanks goes out to the elders of Waitaha, the elders of the Red Earth & the Twelve Indian Nations, the elders of the trails of the Standing Stones, the stone keepers; Ngatapuwae Trust; Barbara; Karen & David, Jason, Moana, Gary & Raywyn, Judi, Tom & Yvonne, El & Ann, Peter & Carol, Ko & Mum, Paul & Wendy; proof readers - Tamzin, Amy, Gillian, Marylyn; readers - Gordon & Bev, Marie & Rudolf, Lynda, Greg & Rose; those who helped open the way, Hamish & Lyn, David & Jenny, Phoebe, Ben & Robyn, Ian & Kay, Heike & Janni, Heidi, Ruth; on the Lake Trail - Viv & Robert, Moana & Jane; trail walkers - Jo, Derek, Caroline, Peter, Gordon, Pere, Katrina, Richard, Petariki, Puke & Margaret; on the Twelve Nations trail - Maru, Wendy, Cornelius & Alan; Ellie, the two Roberts, Ken, Catharine; on the Standing Stone Trail Malcolm & Margaret, Ros & David, Stephanie & Jim & Sydney, Ben, Kevin, Bella & Debbie.

Thankyou to the Ngatihine Forest Trust for permission to share the story of Kauri.

Published by Stoneprint Press
PO Box 12-360, Chartwell
Hamilton,
New Zealand

Designed and illustrated by
Wenetia Publications.
Hamilton

Printed by
Printhouse Ltd. , Hamilton

Film Makers
Bay Scan, Tauranga

Photography for cover & inside pages
Paul Jones

Photograph of author
Jason Busch

Orders for
Song of the Stone
The Tattooed Land
Greenstone Trails
to Stoneprint Press
Fax 07 8552 510, Hamilton

ISBN 0-9583502-0-5

'Be gentle with yourself. You are a child of the universe,
no less than the trees & the stars; you have a right to be here.
And whether or not it is clear to you,
no doubt the universe is unfolding as it should.'

Desiderata 1642

I greet the Source,
I honour the ancestors.
I walk in the light.
I embrace life.
I know my wairua is of the stars and returns
to the stars from whence it came.